Healthy Mourning, Happy Loving

Healthy Mourning, Happy Loving

By Maria Kliavkoff

Dearest Ifunanya –

Wishing you much ease & grace in your grief journey. Knowing the love you are will deliver the love in the journey. Much Love,

M

HM
PUBLICATIONS

Healthy Mourning Publications
Box 282 Radium Hot Springs, BC
Canada V0A 1M0

ISBN 978-1-9992439-0-6

Table of Contents

Acknowledgements

This book could not have been possible without a few key people. My deepest gratitude to you all:

Dr. Alan Wolfelt, my mentor and teacher, you inspire me with your words and actions. Without you, this book would not exist. Your Center for Loss and Life Transition is a gift to the world. Thank you for all you do.

Lana Skauge, my writing buddy. Thank you for the daily contact, the grounding, the words of inspiration and the reminder that we all have something important to say.

Editor, Gayl Veinotte, you were a rock in the storm of my insecurities and an anchor in the ocean of my stories. Thank you for helping me to creating a book that flows with ease and grace.

Graphic artist, Shawn Wernig, you produce images that vibrate with the essence of the ideas and words that have been shared with you. Thank you for helping me to creating a book that vibrates beautifully.

All of you who pick up this book and allow it to support you in transforming your grief to mourning. May you find ease and grace in your journey.

Finally, the information in this book comes from a lifetime of learning and growing. Gratitude to all who have crossed my path including family, friends, clients and colleagues. Thank you for sharing your stories and your wisdom.

Preface

Grieving is one of the hardest processes a human being goes through. The key to getting to the other side is the willingness to go through it and to do the "hard work of mourning," as Dr. Alan Wolfelt calls it.

I was blessed to study with Dr. Wolfelt at the Center for Loss & Life Transition, where I received my Death and Grief Studies Certificate. It was a turning point in my life. For the first time, I learned how to mourn well so that I could go on to live well. I had been burying and carrying grief for decades. Dr. Wolfelt taught me what I needed to do in order to walk through that grief and begin living again.

Towards the end of my studies, my mother became ill and died. In the following year and half, I had the opportunity to put all of my training to personal use, and what I found was this: the more I was able to consciously convert my grief to mourning, the easier the journey became. It is not that I no longer felt the pain, rather it was that I had learned to trust myself. I learned how to listen to my inner knowing and trust the ways I wanted and needed to express my grief and convert it to mourning. I found that with every action and every ritual the symptoms of my grief softened. As I turned inward to listen to and follow my inner guidance, my grief was telling me what to do next. As I followed my intuition, I found moments of relief and release. With time, the heaviness of the grief lifted, and I came through the other side of what was a very dark cave.

This book is a compilation of the strategies I used to convert my grief to mourning. I offer it to you as a companion for your grief journey. Take from it that which speaks to you. Modify any suggestion to the calling of your heart. Only you know the pathway through your grief. Trust what your heart tells you. It knows your truest path to healing. And please know, you are not alone.

May this book bring you the comfort and support you need. May you embrace your tears and your laughter, for they are both healing your hurting heart, and may you find connection in the journey of honouring and remembering your loved one.

Wishing you peace, love, ease and grace on this most sacred of journeys.

Maria
Radium Hot Springs, BC Canada
January, 2019

How To Use This Book

A quick note before we begin on terminology and how to use this book. The terms "grief" and "mourning" are often used interchangeably, so you may have some confusion regarding the precise meaning of these terms. The definition of these terms is as follows:

> **Grief** is the internal constellation of symptoms: physical, emotional, mental, social and spiritual that we experience when we encounter loss.

> **Mourning** is the external expression of the internal experience.

This book is focused on converting grief to mourning. In other words, we consciously work to shift the internal experience into an external expression that releases the symptoms from our body, mind, heart and soul. It is in the act of conversion that we begin to accept our new reality. It is in the reconciliation with the new reality that true healing occurs.

Sir Paul McCartney once equated the grief that he felt for his beloved wife, Linda, with waves that come, "some are gentle, others will take you out." Grief does come in waves. The grief journey is about learning how to honour the waves as they come. It is also about learning how to speak with others so that they can better understand what we are going through. As we find and hone the tools and techniques that convert grief to mourning, so do we discover ease and grace in the journey.

"Death ends a life, but it does not end a relationship."
- Robert Woodruff Anderson

This quote walked me through the hardest and darkest of times after my mother died. Every time someone suggested I needed "closure," I would share the quote and explain that I was in a difficult process of letting go of my mother physically, and discovering where our relationship exists now. This often led to interesting conversations.

You will find in your grief journey that people often don't know what to say or they say things that are not in alignment with what you know to be true. It will be your choice whether to educate them about your journey or to not connect with them for a while in order to give yourself the space you need. In this, as with all things, listen to your inner guidance. You know best what is healing and supportive and what is distracting and potentially harmful to you. Follow your inner knowing.

The book is laid out with 52 suggestions for converting grief to mourning. I have done them all and found them helpful in my journey. This does not mean that you must do all 52, nor does it mean that you must do them in the order laid out. As always, I invite you to trust your inner knowing. If something sounds interesting, do it. If something does not sound right for you, don't do it. Maybe you will find something that sounds right for later, but not now; trust that inner knowing. You may choose to read the book cover to cover or you may choose to have it on your nightstand for reference whenever you need a way to release what is going on inside. Use the book in the way that best supports you.

To help you use this book as a resource I have created a chart, which is at the back of the book. The chart cross references the symptoms of grief (physical, mental, emotional, social and spiritual) and the stage of the grief journey (early, middle or late) with the 52 conversion techniques covered in the book. This will help you quickly find a conversion technique that best supports you in this moment. I have also recorded 52 short videos that are available to you, free of charge, at the Healthy Mourning, Happy Loving Video Library. The videos are intended to be there for you if you are having a hard time concentrating on the book or if you are needing a friendly voice in moments when you feel isolated and alone. To access the library, please go to *http://bit.ly/HMHLVideoLibraryLink*.

And please remember, I know and trust that you know what is best for you right now, even if you are unsure of this truth in this moment. Lean on my trust and continue to listen to your inner guidance. You will get there. It will take time, and that is okay. Grief is a testament to your love. As you honour and celebrate the love you had, so do you move through grief and reclaim both your memories and your love.

1
Symbol of Strength

Grief is not a problem to be solved; it is a process that we go through. The truth is, most people avoid it, because it is hard. Grief brings with it a myriad of physical, mental, emotional, social and spiritual symptoms. Questions range from the basics of self-care and functioning to existential crises of faith. In this turmoil, we need something to ground into and lean on, something to remind ourselves that we have the strength to walk through the process of grief. A symbol of strength can remind us of and connect us to the power we have within.

One of the things I learned from a Native elder many years ago is that the Blackfoot revere the buffalo as the smartest of all animals. Only the buffalo is smart enough to know that when a storm is coming, you turn towards it and walk through it, because that is the shortest time spent in the storm. All other animals, humans included, run from the storm, which only causes them to spend more time in the chaos of the storm. Creator rewards the buffalo with a strong tuft of hair on the forehead to protect this wise creature from the storm it faces. So, too, does the God of our understanding give us the tools we need as we need them. When my mother died, the buffalo became an important symbol for me. I placed a picture of a buffalo where I would see it every day. It was a powerful reminder to face the storms of grief as they appear and to trust that Creator would give me what I need to survive.

Getting Started

- ♥ Begin with getting curious. Ask yourself, "What is my symbol for strength? How can it help me through this difficult time?"

- ♥ Find or create a physical reminder of your symbol of strength

- ♥ Place the symbol somewhere prominent, where you will see it throughout your day.

- ♥ Share the symbol and the story of why it gives you strength with someone you trust.

  - ♡ There is power in sharing your stories with someone else. As you speak to another person about your power symbol, you hear yourself speak. You learn from what you say, and the symbol becomes more meaningful and personal.

  - ♡ Your supportive friend may also have thoughts to share that will give you a greater perspective and appreciation of the benefits of your symbol.

  - ♡ By asking a friend to listen, you give them the opportunity to help. In times of grief, friends often feel helpless; they don't know what to say or do. By asking them to listen to and validate what you are saying, you communicate that you trust them. That trust is a priceless gift.

Join us in the video library for more on this approach to converting grief to mourning. http://bit.ly/HMHLVideoLibraryLink

2
Colour My World

In the early days of grief, we are likely to suffer from symptoms in five areas of our life: physical, mental, emotional, social and spiritual. During this time, our mind is preoccupied with thoughts of our loved one. We can experience a cacophony of noise in our head that will not be silenced and does not allow us to rest. At this time, focusing our attention on a singular task like colouring can be helpful. Colouring distracts us temporarily from the cacophony and helps us to gently engage with our emotions. Colouring mandalas can help us to feel in control at a time when everything is out of our control. We can begin to bring order to the chaos we are experiencing.

After my father died, my mother and I flew to Bulgaria, to bury his ashes. As I was leaving my house for the airport, I ran upstairs to grab my mandala book, my coloured pencils and my markers. I'm so grateful that I followed this impulse. On the plane, I opened the book and began colouring; in the hotel in Bulgaria I coloured; when I could not sleep I coloured. When I had no words to express the depth and breadth of the emotions I was feeling, I would pull out the book and the pencils. Sometimes, I pressed hard on the pencil, and sometimes, I could barely lift it. Slowly, the emotions released their grip and words would emerge. I wrote the words on the page and continued to colour. It allowed me a safe place to connect with and release my thoughts and feelings. It was a life line in the early days of my grief.

Getting Started

- ♥ Gather together a mandala book, coloured pencils, markers and / or paints — whatever speaks to you.

- ♥ Begin by finding a mandala that resonates for you. Don't overthink this; just choose one that feels right to you.

- ♥ Choose colours that feel appropriate. While we tend to like bright, happy colours, don't be surprised if you gravitate to other darker or muted colours at this time. This is an exploration and an opportunity to express on paper what you are honestly thinking and feeling. Follow your instincts, including the choice of design and colour. Your inner self knows what you need. Trust what it is prompting you to choose. You can always do another one with brighter colours later, when that feels true.

- ♥ Most mandala books have blank circles at the back so that you can draw your own mandala of grief. This is a powerful tool. Put your pencil on the paper and just begin drawing. You may be surprised at what comes out.

- ♥ If a mandala doesn't call to you, find whatever works for you. It may be a blank page; it may be a colouring book. Trust your inner knowing; only you know what is right for you.

Join us in the video library for more on this approach to converting grief to mourning. http://bit.ly/HMHLVideoLibraryLink

3
Picture This

The importance of photos cannot be overstated. In the early days of grief, we are asked to find a picture to use for obituaries, memorial cards, remembrance montages, grave stones and the like. This initial search for individual pictures can be an important part of the grieving process. It opens the floodgates to memory. The stories and memories help us feel connected once again with those we love. The pictures offer an opportunity to explore and learn about the story of the life that has just ended.

For both my mother and my father, I created a photo montage of their life for their memorial services. For my father, I created two videos, one of his early years and one of his life with my mother and his family. The photo montages were then set to music. For my mother, I created a slideshow of her life that I narrated. Both approaches required me to go through the pictures and select the moments that I knew were meaningful to them. This exercise allowed me to get to know them better. It was the true beginning of my grief process and my healing journey.

Getting Started

- ♥ When you close your eyes and picture your loved one, is there a particular photo that comes to mind? This is likely the picture you want to use for the obituary and memorial card, because this is the one that represents their truest essence to you.

- ♥ Once you find it, you may want to create a larger print of the photo and frame it so that you can use it at a funeral or memorial service and then later display it on a home altar.

- ♥ Going through a lot of pictures and picking just a few to use can be overwhelming, but it can also be comforting. Take your time. Enjoy the memories. If possible, share this experience with others who are able to share their memories of your loved one with you.

- ♥ Enjoy the pictures you have never seen before. Ask family and friends to share their pictures and memories with you. (This may occur over a long period of time.) In this way, you can learn about aspects of your loved one that you never knew.

- ♥ If your insides are telling you that this is too painful and you need to get rid of all your pictures, take your time packing them carefully and intentionally. If you cannot do this, ask a friend or family member to do it for you. There will likely come a time in the future when you will be ready to bring the photos back. Allow yourself the time and the space to be able to do this with intention and honour.

Join us in the video library for more on this approach to converting grief to mourning. http://bit.ly/HMHLVideoLibraryLink

4
Sleepless and Restless

Sleep disturbance is a recognized physical symptom of grief. This symptom can cause frustration. Unsure what to do, we listen to the clock tick and agonize over lost sleep along with all our other losses. While it is true that every symptom of grief is designed to slow us down and bring our awareness to the present moment, this can feel more threatening in the wee hours and can become exacerbated if we wake in a state of anxiety or panic.

Normalizing the symptom can help us to accept it for the time being. Depending on where we are with our grief, it is important to go gently with ourselves, dosing if we need to and orienting ourselves to what needs to be released when appropriate.

After my father died, I always woke at 4 a.m. When talking with a friend, she mentioned that she used to do the same thing. Even though her father was sick for years, after he died, she no longer felt protected and safe. The next morning when I woke at 4 a.m., I said aloud, "I wonder if I am not feeling safe?" I closed my eyes and took a deep breath. I felt my father in the room. I also felt a deep peace come over me. I fell asleep immediately and awoke later truly rested. Sometimes, naming it is all we need to do.

There are many ways to soften the symptoms of sleeplessness and restlessness.

Getting Started

- ♥ Keep water by your bedside. This helps stave off dehydration. It also helps to reground and slow down your racing head so that you can become more present to the moment.

- ♥ Keep a box of tissues at your bedside. Early morning cries can release a lot of tension from your mind and body.

- ♥ Keep a pad of paper and pen at your bedside to record any dreams or thoughts you have that may be keeping you up.

- ♥ Become aware of your surroundings and reorient yourself. (Be gentle with yourself as you do this. In the early days of grief, this can also mean remembering the loss.)

- ♥ If you are not comfortable lying in bed, get out of bed, walk around, write in your journal or put on some music. Listen to your inner guidance. What does it want you to do?

- ♥ If you find yourself waking with anxiety, you can:

  - ♡ Focus on your breathing and begin to consciously slow it down by counting as you breathe in and out, varying the count as you go. (e.g., breathe in 1-2-3, breathe out 1-2-3-4.)

  - ♡ Take a drink of water to help ground yourself and regulate your system.

  - ♡ Massage your earlobes and your temples.

  - ♡ If your brain is racing with thoughts, write them out on a piece of paper.

Join us in the video library for more on this approach to converting grief to mourning. http://bit.ly/HMHLVideoLibraryLink

5
Linking Objects

Linking objects have a powerful ability to support us in our healing journey. A linking object is a physical object that belonged to our loved one and now is in our possession. Every time we see it, hear it, smell it, wear it or engage with it, it reminds us of them. Sometimes, a linking object is important in the early days of grief and drops away over time, while others remain with us for our lifetime. Linking objects bring comfort and support, because they remind us of the physical presence of our loved one.

When my mother died and we were packing her apartment, it was hard to choose which objects to keep. I had identified a couple of key objects, but I was overwhelmed with clothes, blankets, clocks, furniture and jewelry. The jewelry I put in a box and decided to distribute among family members at a later date. Much to my surprise, I discovered the most important item was a clock that was given to my father when he retired. The clock chimes every hour. I have heard that clock through good times and bad during visits in my parents' home in Seattle. I shared a room with the clock throughout my mother's final weeks. I brought the clock to my home in Canada. There are times when I hear the clock clearly no matter where I am in the house. In those moments, I smile. Sometimes, a tear slips down my cheek, but always, I feel an energetic hug from beyond.

Getting Started

- ♥ Choose linking objects that support your needs. The key is in the meaning that it holds and the comfort that it brings you.

  - ♡ It may be an article of clothing, such as a scarf, shirt, jacket, robe — anything that holds the scent of your loved one.

  - ♡ Perhaps it is a special object that you used with them or that you purchased together.

  - ♡ Maybe it's a piece of jewelry or a watch, something that they wore regularly. The possibilities are endless.

- ♥ If you are responsible for distributing objects left behind, you may want to ask family members and friends if there is anything specific that has meaning for them that they would like. Being generous with linking objects opens an opportunity for shared dialogue, memories and converting grief to mourning.

- ♥ As important as it is to have linking objects, it is equally important to allow them to fall away when you no longer need them. The purpose of converting grief to mourning is to discover and accept where the new relationship is. As we claim the new connection, the pain lessens and the physical reminder may no longer be as important as it once was. Allowing the physical to fall away does not mean we love them less; it means we have found where the love lives now.

Join us in the video library for more on this approach to converting grief to mourning. http://bit.ly/HMHLVideoLibraryLink

6
Honour and Altar

Creating a designated area in the home for an altar is a beautiful way to honour our loved ones and keep their presence close. Having pictures and memorabilia around, particularly in the early days of grief, can be a great comfort. The process of selecting pictures and items for the altar helps to ground the reality of the death. Selecting a spot in the home, or a place outside where we can go and consciously be with our loved one helps to shift the relationship from the physical to where it lives now. Devoting a place to honour their memory and filling that spot with items and photos connects you with them and can help to bridge the loneliness. As time passes, the altar may change, and that is okay. Altars reflect our process, and as the relationship shifts from the physical, so does the altar shift. Allowing the altar to change over time is evidence of moving through the grieving process. Altars can be particularly helpful if we are grieving more than one death at a time.

A month and a half after my mother died, one of my best friends died. I had just begun to create the altar for my mother in my house when I was given the news about my friend. I ended up creating a second altar for my friend in a different part of the house. Half a year later, I felt drawn to bring the two altars together. On the one-year anniversary of my friend's death, the altar was moved to a different part of the house and made into a picture table of those I love, both living and dead. It is a table where I honour all who have influenced me and touched my heart. I love having all the pictures there, in the living room. Every now and then, my eyes fall on one of the pictures that was once on the altar. As I look at the picture, I feel loved and supported. It reminds me that our loving connection is still strong.

Getting Started

- ♥ To make an altar in your home:

  - ♡ Choose a spot in your home where you can devote space to the memory of your loved one.
  - ♡ You may choose to cover the area with a special tablecloth or fabric that holds special meaning for you.
  - ♡ Select your favourite pictures and put them in beautiful frames for display.
  - ♡ Select items that were special to your loved one or remind you of them.
  - ♡ You may want to include flowers, candles, a memorial card and/or an urn.
  - ♡ Arrange the photos and items in a way that is appealing to you and welcoming to all who see it.

- ♥ Possibilities for an altar in another location:

  - ♡ Gravesite or columbarium
  - ♡ Memorial bench, tree, garden
  - ♡ Memorial Facebook page

Join us in the video library for more on this approach to converting grief to mourning. http://bit.ly/HMHLVideoLibraryLink

7
Burning Candles

Using candles to connect with departed loved ones is a long-held tradition in many cultures and world religions. Candles are a gentle and loving way for us to stay present to our process of grief. Because lit candles bring a sense of calm and peace, they create a safe space for reflection.

I was 13 years old when my grandmother, my best friend and confidant, died after an 11-year battle with cancer. In the months following her passing, when I had no words to express my sadness and no friends to talk about it with, I developed a habit that brought me comfort. Every night, before going to bed, I would light a big candle she had given me. The first night, after a month of staring at it on my shelf, I took it down, carefully took off its protective plastic wrap and lit it. I remember sitting next to it, staring at the flame and feeling peace wash over me. I didn't know where that peace came from, but I knew that I slept better that night. So, the next night I lit it again. At first it was five minutes, eventually it grew into a half hour ritual. I would light the candle and begin to talk with my grandmother the way I used to talk with her before she died. When I blew out the candle, I would imagine the smoke was delivering my words to her, wherever she was. It would be a decade before I learned of wisdom traditions worldwide that use the same technique. I was just following my inner guidance. Instinctively, I seemed to know what would bring me peace and comfort.

Getting Started

- Burn a remembrance candle

    - A remembrance candle is a special taper lit in the home over a period of time following the death, lit in a place of worship, or lit on an altar or at a gravesite.
    - Select a candle that has special meaning. As you light the candle, remind yourself that this candle is being lit to help transition your relationship from the physical to the spiritual realm.

- Burn a marriage candle

    Since the vow is "until death do us part," many spouses have found comfort in burning the remaining portion of the marriage candle at designated times. You decide what would have meaning for you.

    - Every evening at a certain time
    - On weekends
    - On special occasions (i.e., birthdays and / or anniversaries)

- Find a special vessel for your special candle

    The candleholder or plate may be a linking object. Place the candle in a prominent position in your house. It may be on your altar, in the window, or on the fireplace. Feel for the right place so that even when it is not burning, it can catch your eye and touch your heart.

Join us in the video library for more on this approach to converting grief to mourning. http://bit.ly/HMHLVideoLibraryLink

8

Creating Your Wellness Team

Grief is not a journey that we go on alone. Since it is likely that our family has also been impacted by this loss, they may not be able to be part of our wellness team, as they are going through their own loss. Identifying who we can call when we need support is crucial.

Traditional wisdom tells us that those closest to us will fall into one of three categories. One third will be neither helpful nor harmful. One third will be harmful, not because they intend to do harm, but because they are misinformed about the grief journey and they do not know how to be there for others in a supportive way. The good news is that one third will know how to be there and are willing to support our journey. This is the group to focus on. They may not be the people we would have thought would be there, but they are showing up now and they are a great help. These are the people we want to keep close.

When my mother first died, I trusted, hoped and believed that my family would be there for me. It was a heartbreak to discover that many of them could not be. I realized that while many people loved me, they could neither support me nor be an emotionally safe place for me. I decided to surround myself with people who could and would walk with me in my grief journey. I chose people who understood what I was going through, knew that it was important for me to not hide my feelings and who would be okay with silence. The people who stayed by my side during that time have become my nearest, dearest and most trusted family, friends and colleagues.

It is important to create wellness teams in all areas where we may need expertise and support.

Getting Started

- ♥ **Body** — massage, reiki, chiropractic and/or medical

- ♥ **Social** — family, neighbours, colleagues and/or friends

- ♥ **Emotional** — bereavement support group, peer support group, hospice or other volunteer support, grief counselor and/or grief coach

- ♥ **Spiritual** — advisor, minister, congregation and/or bereavement support group

- ♥ **Practical** — lawyer, financial (bank contact, accountant, advisor(s), insurance)

Once you identify the individuals and ensure they are part of the helpful third:

- ♥ Create a contact list of names and numbers.

- ♥ Put it in a place (like on the fridge) where you can find it easily when you need it.

- ♥ Use it as needed!

Join us in the video library for more on this approach to converting grief to mourning. http://bit.ly/HMHLVideoLibraryLink

9
Phone a Friend

It is one thing to have a wellness list of people we can call; it is quite another thing to actually call them when we need to. It requires a certain amount of courage, strength and willingness to be vulnerable. This can only occur if we have people we can trust. How we select the people to call was covered in the last chapter. When to call them is simple: whenever we need to. If you are feeling lonely, call. If you are feeling angry, call. If you are feeling desperate, call. If you are feeling numb, call. If you don't know what to say, call. If you are lost, call. If you need to cry, call. A friend will understand. A friend will be there to love and nurture you. A friend will not judge you. A friend will recognize that you honour them with your vulnerability and that you gift them with your tears. When you need to, call.

Ten days after what would have been my mother's 80th birthday, a month and a half after she died, one of my best friends unexpectedly died. I was numb and lost. I had pushed through the day's work (which included teaching the first day of a course on complicated grief). Following the workshop, I contacted the family and was as present for them as I could be. When I hung up with them, I needed love and support. I had tapped out my friends with the loss of my mother. Who could I call now? I gazed at my wellness group list and my eyes dropped to just the right person. I called. She was asleep, and still she welcomed my call. That night she was a lifeline for me. I may never be able to repay her for her kindness to me, but I will be able to pay it forward. And the memory of this moment will live with me forever. This is what friendship is and does. In the moments when we need them most, our truest friends step up in ways we can never imagine. What a gift it is they give us. And what a gift it is we share with them, these precious moments of our lives.

Getting Started

When calling a friend:

- ♥ Honour their time by asking if they have time or could make time for you.

- ♥ Ask them for what you need, especially if what you need is for them to sit in silence with you.

- ♥ Be honest with them about how you feel (including any insecurity you have about sharing your tears and your vulnerability with them, or fearing that they will get tired of hearing you talk.)

- ♥ It is also important to share any push back on advice being given.

- ♥ Allow their words to comfort you.

- ♥ Express your gratitude for them being a safe space for you.

Join us in the video library for more on this approach to converting grief to mourning. http://bit.ly/HMHLVideoLibraryLink

10
The Importance of Nap Time

NAP = Need A Pause

Naps are a wonderful reminder that we need a pause in our day. When grief is fresh, we may discover we are so physically tired that all we can do is lie down. This is a natural response to grief. Our bodies feel weighed down by the heaviness and the aches and pains we are carrying. The need for a nap is our body's way of telling us to slow down. It is an invitation to restore our energy — energy that we cannot afford to expend at this time. With time, and conscious attention, the heaviness lightens and the tiredness lifts, but only if we heed the warnings and follow the body's direction. This is a crucial time to teach our body, our heart and our mind that we are listening to their cues and we are willing to follow their lead.

In the days immediately following my mother's death, I found myself lying in her bed at different times of the day. I would smell her blanket and her pillow and I would drift off. Somehow, that time gave me the connection to her I needed and the strength to get up and do the next thing on what seemed a never-ending list of things that had to get done. One year after her death, I still experienced times when I needed to follow my inner guidance to lie down and take a minute or a half hour. Following this guidance was the difference between struggling against my grief and relaxing into it.

Getting Started

- ♥ Listen to your body's request for rest. When you feel too tired to go on, take time to nap; it is restorative to the body, mind and heart. It brings peace and calm.

- ♥ People may avoid naps because they are afraid that if they lie down, their emotions might "catch up to them." That can be very scary. It is true that when you lie down, you may feel a wave of sadness. Your body is asking you to allow the wave to come and the tears to fall. Having the quiet time and space to express the feelings safely helps you to release what is caught on the inside and to feel relief from the tension and the anxiety of trying to hold it all in.

- ♥ A nap does not mean you need to fall asleep. Sometimes, taking the time — even just 10 minutes — to lay your head on a pillow and wrap yourself in a blanket is all you need to feel supported and nurtured.

- ♥ If you wake from a nap and your body feels very heavy, do not rush to get up. Listen to your body. Talk with it. Ask what it needs. It may just need a little more time before the heaviness can lighten enough for you to get up again.

Join us in the video library for more on this approach to converting grief to mourning. http://bit.ly/HMHLVideoLibraryLink

11

Permission to Dose

Grief can be overwhelming, and it is important to take time away from it when needed. Dosing means that we convert grief to mourning little bits at a time; we don't try to do it all at once. The truth is, we cannot do it all at once. When it becomes too much, our bodies and minds naturally dose.

Dosing gives us time and space, so that our mind, our emotions and our bodies can begin to catch up with all that has occurred. To do this well, we need to trust our natural instincts. Following our inner guidance is key. We need to allow ourselves to act out of character, to do things that distract us from the enormity of what has occurred.

In the months following my father's death, I began eating oatmeal for breakfast. I had not done this since I was a child, when Dad made it for me with honey. Suddenly, I found myself craving this. What began as a way to connect with him over breakfast soon gave way to my craving oatmeal at odd times throughout the day. A good friend told me not to worry about it, to trust my craving. And she was right. The cravings eventually went away, but at the time they were a lifeline. When emotions became too much to bear, the comforting bowl of oatmeal soothed my nerves and allowed me to rest on the inside.

Getting Started

- ♥ Eat comforting foods (grief time is not a time to start or maintain a diet. There will be time for that later, if necessary).

- ♥ Have the television or radio on for white noise (even if it is on all night).

- ♥ Allow yourself to become busy or distracted with a project.

A note of warning with dosing. Dosing becomes avoidance when we do these things not because our inner self tells us to, but as a way to avoid our grief. We know we are doing this when:

- ♥ It no longer feels right to do the activity (particularly if you have never done it before). Dosing activities last for short periods of time. When the activity no longer feels right, you need to get honest with yourself and ask yourself, "Is it still true for me to do this?"

- ♥ If symptoms of grief become more pronounced, it is a warning sign that you are avoiding your grief. Instead of softening over time, grief symptoms seem to be hardening. For example:

  - ♡ Physical aches and pains become stronger.
  - ♡ Mental confusion makes daily tasks harder to accomplish.
  - ♡ Waves of emotion become stronger and harder to contain or hide.
  - ♡ We feel the need to isolate ourselves more.
  - ♡ We feel more spiritual longing.

Dosing is not meant to block our grief; it is meant to give us a respite from grief as we continue on our journey.

Join us in the video library for more on this approach to converting grief to mourning. http://bit.ly/HMHLVideoLibraryLink

12
Connecting with What Connects Us

Love and loss is all about the loss of our sense of connection to our loved one. For some of us, we are so used to having them in the physical realm and we miss them so much, it does not occur to us that the connection is still there. For others, we so long for the connection that we search for it everywhere and feel lost when it does not show up the way we want or expect it to. Where does the relationship live now? How do we connect with what connects us?

About seven months after my mother died, I was driving home from work. The entire time, I was thinking about how I wished I could call her the way I used to. I arrived home. It was a dark, cold and quiet winter night. I wondered what I could do to feel connected with her. I decided I would look at pictures after dinner. What began with an album of pictures became a box of pictures, many of which I had not seen in a long time. I really enjoyed my trip down memory lane. There were tears and laughter as I remembered the story behind every picture. I decided to frame some of them, because I wanted them to be in my living space. It felt good to catch a glimpse of them as I was coming in or heading out the door. Those pictures became a touchstone for me and tethered me to the memories of my mother. This was a vital stepping stone en route to discovering where our relationship is now.

Getting Started

- ♥ In times of loneliness and sadness, the things that connect us are the things that still hold meaning for us.

- ♥ In the early stages of grief, it can be hard to remember what these things are. Creating a list that we can go to when we are missing our loved one can be very helpful.

- ♥ Many things can still help us feel connected to our loved one.

  - ♡ Pictures
  - ♡ Videos and home movies
  - ♡ Song lists
  - ♡ Clothes
  - ♡ Memorabilia
  - ♡ Hobbies (gardening, cooking, woodworking …)
  - ♡ Sports (swimming, tennis, fishing, soccer, baseball, football, hockey …)
  - ♡ Games (chess, backgammon, bridge, rummy-o, mah-jong, video games …)

Join us in the video library for more on this approach to converting grief to mourning. http://bit.ly/HMHLVideoLibraryLink

13
Our Story in Song

Nothing is a quicker memory trigger than music. The lyrics and rhythms transport us instantly to special moments of our lives.

Our reaction to music is visceral and immediate. In the early days of grief, we may need a buffer to protect ourselves from music that pops up on the radio and takes us by surprise. We may find that we cannot listen to the radio at all, because we fear being "taken out" or "flattened" by a song that just happens to pop on as we are on our way to work. If this is a concern, we must give ourselves permission to turn off the radio.

Songs can also provide the pathway to healing. After my friend, Christine, died, one of her favourite songs kept playing in my head (Neil Diamond's "Story of My Life"). One day, I decided to go to our special place in the Canadian Rockies, and I played it on my way there. When I got out of the car and started hiking, I kept hearing the phrase, "It's the story of our times, and never letting go, and if I die today, I wanted you to know." When I sat where we used to sit and reflected on the words, a flood of memories came. As I embraced each memory, the tears came, and so did the longing and the love. The words in the song reminded me to reclaim each cherished memory. Sitting with the song allowed me to access and release many tears, and in so doing I was able to reclaim the memories.

Getting Started

- Selecting the music for a funeral, memorial service or photo montage requires you to:

  - Compile a list of their favourite songs — the songs they sang along with, played continuously or that you associate with them.

  - Take your time doing this. Allow the emotions and memories to come. It is all part of converting grief to mourning in healthy ways.

  - Ask family and friends to send song suggestions. Doing this will support them in their grief journey. You may also learn things you never knew about your loved one, or be reminded of moments you had forgotten about.

- Give yourself permission to cry as you hear the music. It is a healthy thing to do.

- If the song ends and you are not done crying, play it again. Let the tears flow. There is gentleness in no longer fighting to hold the tears in.

- Borrowed tears – sometimes, we need a "tear jerker" song to release the tears that are inside. Finding music that you can turn to when you need to release a few tears is a blessing. One of my favourites is Amy Bishop's "Remembered."

- Share a special song with a trusted friend who can listen to the song with you and also listen to your story.

Join us in the video library for more on this approach to converting grief to mourning. http://bit.ly/HMHLVideoLibraryLink

14
Going Through the Stuff — a Treasure Hunt

With death comes time to clear the belongings of the person who died. While this can be an overwhelming task, it can also be cathartic. Going through our loved one's belongings affords us an opportunity to get to know them better than we ever imagined. The letters, notes, day-timers and journals they left behind are priceless windows into their thoughts and beliefs.

A word of warning, however: this is a process in and of itself. It is not a one-and-done job that can or should be done in a day or two. The discoveries we make can put us on a rollercoaster of memories and emotions in a condensed period of time. The pressure to get it all done when we barely have the energy to lift our arms can be overwhelming. How do we approach this in a way that is supportive of our grief journey and still gets the job done? It is a tall order, yet it is all doable if we follow our inner guidance.

As I thought about all of my Mom's stuff, and all that would need to be packed and moved and given away and, and, and — I quickly became overwhelmed. My friends were coming to help with the task in two days. Meanwhile, I was there, alone in her apartment. I cherished this time of being with her through her stuff. Her artwork. Her office. Her bed. Her, everywhere. I walked into her closet and knew this was where I needed to begin.

And so the piles began. Things I knew I would give away came out first. Some I tried on, just so I could smell her scent. Some I knew I would keep and packed for travel. And then came the I-don't-know pile. I wasn't ready to make a decision about that stuff. It was too much. So, I sat on her bed. I cried a bit. And then I had a brilliant idea: pack what I am not ready to go through yet and label it clearly. It was a year before I was ready to go through the bin. It was the time I needed. A year later, I was ready to let go of most of it.

Getting Started

- ♥ Allow yourself the time and space you need to pack things in a respectful way, even if you don't come back to it for another year.

- ♥ Ask family and friends to help you with the task. Doing so allows you to share stories and discoveries as you work, and it helps to lighten the burden.

- ♥ Have enough air tight, see-through containers (not just boxes), so that clothing and other objects can be packed away, but not hidden. You can see what is in the containers so that later on you can choose which containers you are ready to work with and work through.

Join us in the video library for more on this approach to converting grief to mourning. http://bit.ly/HMHLVideoLibraryLink

15
Words to Live By

Finding the words that held meaning for our loved one gives us an opportunity to discover who they were. If we are lucky, we find these words before they die and we can discuss them. Other times, we only find the words as we go through their belongings following their death. Either way, the words help us understand what our loved ones valued, who they aspired to be and how they saw the world. These words bring greater understanding and appreciation for who they were and offer comfort and clarity to us as we begin to move forward in our lives.

While packing my father's belongings to go to the nursing home, I found a beautiful poem that was sent to him in the 1970s. It was something he kept in his desk with his favourite pictures, so I knew how important it was to him. The poem was a reworking of "'Twas The Night Before Christmas," written for soldiers. It helped me understand his pride at having been a soldier who defended his country in WWII and his loyalty and dedication to the armed services. It helped me understand him. A few weeks before his death, I knelt at his bedside and read the poem out loud. I began to cry as I was reading. When the tears clouded my eyes so badly that I could no longer read, he reached out to touch me. In that moment we connected in a way we had never connected before. He knew that I saw him and I understood.

Days after my mother died, I found a re-wording of the Serenity Prayer in her handwriting. She wrote it in 1959. The words she chose were uniquely her own, and I understood something about my mother, who she was and how she lived her life. I felt a wave of appreciation and respect wash over me. Though she wasn't physically there, I felt a hand on my arm, the way my father had touched me, and I knew that she knew.

Getting Started

Finding the words that were so precious to our loved one may be easier than we think.

- ♥ Is there a favourite quote from a book that is written on the refrigerator or displayed on their bathroom mirror, dresser or nightstand?

- ♥ Is there a poster or picture with a saying that hung in their home or office?

- ♥ Is there a hand-written note, specialty card or coin in their wallet?

- ♥ Is there a special book on their nightstand with notes in the margin, highlighted or underlined sections?

- ♥ As you find the words that held special meaning for your loved one, sit with the words. Read them out loud. Take time to contemplate and reflect on them. How did these words inform or guide your loved one's choices? What guidance do these words offer you?

Join us in the video library for more on this approach to converting grief to mourning. http://bit.ly/HMHLVideoLibraryLink

16
Journal It — Write It Out

Journaling is not for everyone. Even for those who like to write, journaling — particularly every day — can be challenging while grieving. Journaling, however, is a wonderful way to convert grief to mourning, because it expresses what we are thinking onto a page. It allows space and breath for the multitude of emotions and thoughts to be released. We need not hold ourselves to a rigid schedule of journaling; we need only find what works.

Though I am an avid journaler, I found it challenging to put pen to paper in the early days of my grief. Eventually, I began a new journal. Every day I wrote answers to the following questions:

1. What does love want me to know today?

2. How is life loving me today?

3. What is one thing I can do to help life love me even more?

I found these questions by trusting and following my inner guidance. Early in my grief journey, I felt directed to the writings and Facebook video blogs of Hay House author Robert Holden and the Facebook Group: Presence of Love hosted by Hollie Holden. The questions came from a particular video blog where Robert posed these questions to the group. I immediately resonated with the questions and knew they were a pathway for me. After a few months, I added a gratitude list to the bottom of these questions. The journal became a way for me to check in with myself every day. This helped me to navigate through the muck of my grief and focus on the love. I encourage you to explore your inner guidance and discover what works best for you.

Getting Started

- ♥ **Artistic journal** – Assemble poems, quotes and pictures that inspire you. You can reply to or engage with that which inspires you and record your thoughts and feelings.

- ♥ **Mourning pages** (inspired by Julia Cameron's Morning Pages from her book The Artist's Way) – Whenever you feel locked in your grief and unable to access your thinking or feeling, simply put pen to page and start writing. "I don't know how to do this…I am so frustrated…" Keep writing until you feel a shift. That includes a shift that frees some tears.

- ♥ **Understanding Your Grief Book and Companion Journal** by Dr. Alan Wolfelt is a terrific resource that can help you understand the journey you are on. The journal asks key questions that can help unearth and normalize your thoughts, feelings and beliefs about the death and about what you have experienced since the death of your loved one.

- ♥ **Remembrance book or scrapbook** – Collections of photos and/or stories from you and others that become a compilation of your loved one's life for generations to come. This is a lovely project for the whole family that helps everyone share their stories and convert their grief to mourning.

Join us in the video library for more on this approach to converting grief to mourning. http://bit.ly/HMHLVideoLibraryLink

17
Message in a Bottle

In days of yore, sailors would take to the seas, and their wives, girlfriends and children would write letters, put them in a bottle and release them into the sea in the hope their loved one would find the message and feel their love.

Finding ways to communicate our love with the person who has died is vital in our healing process. It is how we begin to reconnect. By finding a method that works for us, we find a way to sit with our thoughts and feelings, express them, and release them. This is about discovering how to continue the dialogue despite the obvious challenges. We discover ways to communicate our thoughts and feelings, and we begin to believe that our words are being received by our beloved. As time passes, we realize the method of communicating is less of a physical act. In the first year, the physical may feel more appropriate. The important thing is that we follow our inner guidance and do what is right for us.

When I returned home from Seattle, someone — to this day I do not know who — sent me a beautiful basket of plants with a pink butterfly, one black marker, seven helium balloons and a note that instructed me to write a note once a day for the next week to my mother and release it. I decided to keep the balloons; they made my heart happy. Every day I wrote a note to my mother and at the end of the day I burned the note in a smudge bowl out on my deck. I watched as the paper turned to ash and the smoke rose. The ritual of this practice every evening for one week helped me to ground into the realization that my Mother's body, like the paper I was burning, had been reduced to ashes; yet her Spirit, like the smoke, had gone somewhere, and I was working to discover how to connect with that.

Getting Started

- ♥ Write a letter(s).

  - ♡ Place the letter(s) in a special vessel that you buy for just this purpose. You may put them in a box or canister on your altar.

  - ♡ Place the letter in the burial vault, casket or with the ashes when they are buried. You can invite every member of the family to write their own letter.

  - ♡ Burn it. Many cultures believe the smoke from that which is burned carries the words to our loved ones.

- ♥ Have a conversation.

  - ♡ Talk to your loved one, in the shower, in the car, any place where you feel close.

  - ♡ Choose a regular time to connect.

Join us in the video library for more on this approach to converting grief to mourning. http://bit.ly/HMHLVideoLibraryLink

18
Messages and Meaning

My dear friend, musician Eileen McGann, in her haunting song, "Let There Be Angels," wrote the beautiful line, "If there be angels, won't you drop me a feather today?"

When a loved one dies, we look for signs everywhere. We look for signs that they are okay, signs that we will be okay. We hope for messages and put meaning and significance onto what may be insignificant events in other people's eyes. Feathers in our path, a blue sky with a heart or angel cloud formation, heart stones, butterflies on our path all carry significance for those who see the event and give meaning to it. Meaning is personal. It is our interpretation that gives significance and meaning to an event. It is important that we not allow others to minimize our experiences, particularly if the event brings us comfort and peace. The meaning that we give these events is our way of coping with that which seems impossible to digest.

In the weeks leading up to my Mother's passing, we occasionally talked of butterflies. I even bought a butterfly pin in her favourite colour that came with a note that said, "Every time I see a butterfly, I will think of you." She smiled at the idea that we would be able to communicate after she was physically gone. The day after she died, I was walking in a park and the biggest butterfly I have ever seen came charging at me, flew around me two times and then flew away.

It seemed to me this was my mother's way of telling me

she was okay. It had to be Mom because I felt so targeted by this butterfly. In truth, who knows what was going on? All I know is, I felt comforted by the thought that all was well with her and that she found a way to let me know. Since that time, I have seen butterflies and found feathers at the most amazing locations at the perfect moments. Messages are everywhere, if I choose to see them and am willing to be comforted by them.

Getting Started

- Be open to the places you may find messages — the possibilities are endless.

  - In the clouds

  - A feather at your feet

  - Butterflies in your path

  - A flower

  - A chill that runs through your body

  - An object moved

  - A lost object found

  - A vision

  - A dream

- Honour the message when you see it by

  - Recording the experience in a journal.

  - Sharing the experience with a friend.

  - Expressing gratitude for the experience.

Join us in the video library for more on this approach to converting grief to mourning. http://bit.ly/HMHLVideoLibraryLink

19
Drumming the Heartbeat

There is nothing more powerful than the sound of a hand drum beating the rhythm of the heartbeat. The heartbeat is a slow, sturdy, strong beat that we recognize as home, and it works to calm us.

Sometimes, after a loved one dies, we find that we question the beating of our own heart; I know I did. It took a long time for me to find that heartbeat again. Occasionally, I would tap the rhythm with my hand. I found it nurturing and soothing; it gave me a sense of calm and connection to my inner self, even when I couldn't feel the connection.

The metaphor of the heartbeat became so meaningful for me, that when it came time to bury my mother's ashes, I chose to have a drum circle. Everyone in attendance had rattles and drums, and we collectively beat the heartbeat as the gentleman came to place the stone in front of the vault with the ashes, letter and pictures. As the stone went into place, we stopped drumming and there was silence. It was a moment I will never forget. It was the next step in reconciling myself to the truth that my mother no longer had a heartbeat. She was no longer in the physical realm. Now she lived in our hearts and in our memories.

Getting Started

- ♥ Start drumming. You can use anything to drum out a beat, your hands clapping, on a table, desk or box, shaking a rattle, or snapping your fingers.

- ♥ If you find yourself confused or disoriented, it is helpful to use your fingers to beat the rhythm of your heartbeat against your chest. This allows you to release your hard, overworked brain and reconnect with your heart and your body.

- ♥ Beating out the heartbeat is calming and reassuring, but you need not always use the one beat.

- ♥ If you are working with a physical symptom like a back ache or tiredness, you can feel into the symptom and beat out the rhythm of the symptom. As the symptom shifts, so will the sound of the drum.

- ♥ Continue to use this tool to move through physical, mental and emotional symptoms as they come up. It is a gentle way to connect with the grief symptom and convert your grief to mourning.

- ♥ This is especially effective when you work with emotional symptoms. Simply drum the beat of the emotion. Consciously put the emotion into your hands and let your hands release it onto the drum, rattle or table top. You will find as you express the sound of the emotion, the emotion begins to shift. Allow the shift to happen effortlessly and without thought.

- ♥ Attend a drum circle. Facilitators provide the instruments and the guidance; all you need to do is sit and drum. By the end of the evening, you will feel a lightening of your spirit.

Join us in the video library for more on this approach to converting grief to mourning. http://bit.ly/HMHLVideoLibraryLink

20

Take Your Loved One to Tea or Coffee

As we continue to discover ways to reconnect with our loved one and reclaim our relationship with them, it is important that we find ways to be present to and with them. Since part of our brain is working on the question "where are they now," it makes sense that we occasionally take the time to actively pursue the new relationship.

On the first-year anniversary of one of my best friend's death, I asked myself, what would Chris and I do if she were alive today? Where would we go if we wanted to connect and talk with each other? I realized the answer was that we would likely meet at the Starbucks halfway between our houses. So many times, we would call each other up and ask, "Are you free for a cup of tea?" I'd head out the door and walk the three blocks in joyful anticipation of a visit with her. So, on the one-year anniversary, that is what I did. I put my coat on and walked to the Starbucks in anticipation of meeting my friend there. I ordered a tea and a vanilla bean scone, just as we had done so many times. I set an empty chair across from me and, in my mind, I spoke with her. I sat at the table, I felt her presence and I shed a few tears. It was an opportunity for me to work through and talk through all I needed to process. By choosing to return to the place where we had shared so many tears and so much laughter, I allowed things that were inside of me to gently come into my conscious awareness and heal. As always happened when we met in this place, the ah-ha's were so valuable. It was another way for me to explore where the relationship is now and find how to connect with her again. It was a huge step in converting more of my grief to mourning.

Getting Started

- ♥ Create a list of places that you went to together. These are sacred places that hold precious memories.

- ♥ Create a day and time when you will go to one of the places on your list with the intention of meeting your loved one there.

- ♥ Bring anything that would be supportive of having the conversation you need to have with your loved one, anything that will support and not impede your process. It could be a journal or tape recorder. The purpose is to connect with your loved one in a meaningful way, and only you know what that will be.

- ♥ Allow the conversation to unfold naturally.

Join us in the video library for more on this approach to converting grief to mourning. http://bit.ly/HMHLVideoLibraryLink

21
The Healing Nature of Water

Finding ways to sooth the body and the mind during times of grief is important. Our bodies and minds are carrying a tremendous burden right now. Finding ways to nurture our self is key. Warm or cool healing waters may be just what the body longs for. Water grounds us and reminds us that there is a flow to life. Sometimes, it is only in the presence of water that we are able to truly release and let go of our pent-up emotions.

In the days and weeks following my mother's death, with a hundred things to do and think about every waking moment, the shower seemed to be the only safe place for me. I would let the water wash over me. One day, I decided I just wanted to sit in hot water. The only tub was a walk-in, which requires you to be in the tub as the water both collects and drains. Feeling it rise inch by inch, soothing my weary, sore muscles was just the beginning. By the time the tub was full, I felt immersed, protected and cradled — something I had been longing to feel. Tears slid down my cheeks as the memories came and went. It was bittersweet and oh, so gentle. As I pulled the plug and the water level dropped, I felt tired. I was spent and ready for a peaceful sleep. It didn't last all night, but it was peaceful for a few hours — and that meant everything.

Getting Started

- ♥ Let water wash over you. The feeling of water flowing over your face and body is soothing and invites you to remember that you are a part of the flow of life, even if it doesn't feel that way at this time.

- ♥ Take time to assemble everything you need for a soothing bath. As you think about scents, bath salts, candles and music, your body begins to melt into the experience. Running the water and then gently stepping into the environment you created allows you to hand over your worries, even for a short period of time. Step into the hot water and let it soothe your muscles and nurture your soul. Sometimes, gentle memories, quiet thoughts or soft tears surface. Let them. You are safe. This is a wonderful way to convert some of your grief to mourning.

- ♥ Soak in natural hot springs; this is nurturing and nourishing to a weary body, mind, heart and soul. As you linger in the warmth, allow the safety of the water to embrace you. Soak in support from the nature that surrounds you.

- ♥ Go for a swim or dangle your feet in the cool of a natural lake; feel the cool, healing water take your pain. Surrender your pain to this water; the water knows what to do with it.

Join us in the video library for more on this approach to converting grief to mourning. http://bit.ly/HMHLVideoLibraryLink

22
The Challenge of Holidays

Holidays can be a very hard time for those who are grieving. Memories are everywhere, and the longing to have our loved one with us can make the idea of celebrating overwhelming. How do we use the holidays and the feelings they bring up to continue our grief journey when the temptation to run from the feelings and ignore the holiday is so great? As with all other moments in grief, it begins with the earnest intention to move through the grieving process by befriending our grief symptoms and giving our kaleidoscope of emotions an avenue of expression. As the holidays approach, there are key things we can do to help us lean into the experience instead of hiding from them.

The year following my mother's death, I made a conscious choice to do something different for every holiday. I travelled at Thanksgiving and hosted her New York Memorial Service on Wednesday of US Thanksgiving week. At Christmas, I drove for an hour to volunteer with the Golden Interact Club for their Anti-Grinch Campaign. At Easter, I invited my friends over for an Italian dinner.

All the while, I stayed conscious of my feelings. I allowed the travel to open a space where I could connect and stay present to what was really going on. As I drove home from Golden on Christmas Eve, I realized Mom wouldn't be at the other end of a phone when I got home. I would never again get to sing Silent Night with her as we had done the previous year and throughout my childhood. I remembered singing with my Mom over the phone the year before, and a smile cracked through the tears. It was bittersweet. I was devastated that we wouldn't be doing that this year, but at the same time I was so deeply grateful for the memory we created the year before.

Getting Started

- ♥ Remember past holidays – Sharing stories of cherished holiday memories with friends and family helps you empty your hearts and mind, and helps your loved one to live on through the memories and stories.

- ♥ Take an inventory of all of the holiday traditions and choose which to keep and which to let go of based on which traditions bring you joy.

- ♥ What traditions do you choose to let go of? It is possible to cherish the memories, even as we let go of the tradition.

- ♥ If this is a first year after the death and you do not want to deal with the holidays, choose to let it go for this year. You can always choose to return to a tradition in a year or two. For this year, do what feels right for you and give yourself permission to let the rest go.

Join us in the video library for more on this approach to converting grief to mourning. http://bit.ly/HMHLVideoLibraryLink

23

Permission to Create a New Holiday Tradition

Holidays are always challenging, but particularly so if we are grieving a loss. Our memories are tied up with traditions — traditions we miss and dinner tables we will never again know. It can all be overwhelming. Letting go of traditions that no longer feel true and allowing new traditions to evolve is all part of the process. Our willingness to explore the family traditions and discover what remains important will point us in the right direction.

I remember my mother writing Christmas cards, doing Christmas shopping, wrapping presents, making traditional Christmas cakes and other holiday foods of her Hungarian heritage — and I remember her exhaustion, her stress and her frustration.

What gave her joy? Christmas morning brunch. My mother loved a good brunch. So, this became the tradition that I carry forward. The holiday brunch always has my mother's energy imbued in it. When it comes to holiday baking, I found a cookie recipe that tasted like a cookie she loved as a child. It is a cookie she never made, but one that her mother made and the one that I always made for her. After she died, it became important for me to continue to make this cookie. (My friends remain grateful.)

In the first year after my mother died, I decided every holiday I would do something I had never done before, remaining mindful of what felt true for me. I gave money to organizations that had meaning for my mother at Thanksgiving, I volunteered for an organization that reflected her values at Christmas. In this way I participated in activities that allowed me to feel connected to her. This freed me to enjoy the holidays and be present to my grief journey.

Getting Started

- ♥ Reflect on the traditions that do hold meaning for you. What changes can you make to these traditions to make them your own?

- ♥ What would make this holiday special for you? When you listen to your inner prompting, what do you feel called to do? What do you feel called to let go of?

- ♥ Is there an organization that your loved one supported that you would like to support during this holiday season? Will you do it financially? Through volunteer hours? In some other way?

- ♥ What gift did you receive from your loved one? How can you share that gift with someone else this holiday season?

Join us in the video library for more on this approach to converting grief to mourning. http://bit.ly/HMHLVideoLibraryLink

24

A Dinner to Remember

There are foods and flavours that we connect with people in our lives. Even the aroma of favourite meals can trigger powerful memories. Whether they were part of a holiday feast or an everyday staple, they catch us unawares and catapult us into an unexpected burst of grief. It is these occurrences that allow us to convert our grief to mourning in everyday activities, such as cooking dinner in mindful ways.

A number of years ago, I was visiting my mother. My father had died more than a year prior. We were at the market and came across a bin of fresh and beautiful green beans. I smiled, and commented on how Dad loved his green beans. My mother told me that when they were first married, he taught her how to make green beans the way his mother had made them. And so, the stories began. We bought them and everything else we needed to make his special beans. The house was filled with an aroma I had not smelled in a long time. And the stories kept coming. That day is a cherished memory for me. It was my mother and I coming together to convert our grief to mourning. We laughed, we cried, and we ate some really good beans.

Now that my mother has passed, when I need to feel close to her, I cook her favourite foods. I let the aromas hug me from the outside and the familiar flavours hug me on the inside. Most of all, I let the memories, the stories, the tears and the laughter flow.

Getting Started

- ♥ Welcome these sensory culinary moments that bring your grief to the surface. Be willing to share the stories and the memories, however painful, with those close to you.

- ♥ Be present in the healing process as memories are evoked, and recognize that you are being offered yet another invitation to convert grief to mourning.

- ♥ Make a meal of your loved one's favourite foods. Be conscious as you shop, cook and share the flavours with your friends and family.

- ♥ And, as always, stay present to the stories, to the memories and to your feelings.

Join us in the video library for more on this approach to converting grief to mourning. http://bit.ly/HMHLVideoLibraryLink

25
Connecting with Family and Friends

When a beloved family member dies, all family members are affected. We are all grieving and mourning and we all do it in different ways. It is important to give each member the space they need so that we honour each person's grief process.

Sharing memories and stories is a powerful way to support one another as we go through our individual grief journeys. Creating a safe space for both the laughter and the tears allows everyone the opportunity to share what is in their hearts and minds. Sometimes, we need to initiate these stories. We do this by inviting family and friends to share their stories. It is important to be respectful of family members who may not be ready to share. Asking the question "What is your favourite memory of..." can open the door. By listening to other people's stories, we begin to learn things about our loved one that we never knew. We learn about family relationships that we were oblivious to and we learn about everyday things that now become treasures.

One year after my mother died, I began talking with my aunt on the phone regularly. She was my mother's sister-in-law. Her husband, my mother's brother, died at a very young age. Slowly but surely, we began sharing our memories and stories, our tears and our laughter. I learned things about my mother's relationship with her brother and her parents that I never knew. I also learned about my uncle who I cherished. In turn, my aunt discovered new things about her husband and sister-in-law. I was able to participate in the conversion of grief to mourning that had waited 30 years to be released. When we consciously convert grief to mourning for the most recent family death, we create opportunities to do some much needed catch up mourning. It is a beautiful gift.

Getting Started

- Browse through old family photo albums or loose photos with friends or family members. Starting a conversation can be as simple as asking, "Where was this photo taken?"

- When you are with family, particularly for holidays or family celebrations like birthdays or anniversaries, you can use the occasion as a springboard for conversation.

    - "What was Grandpa's favourite holiday?"

    - "What is your favourite holiday memory of Dad?"

    - "Mom loved family birthdays. Do you remember when she…?"

    - "Uncle loved to ring in the New Year in style. What is the craziest New Year's Eve you ever spent together?"

    - "I remember, to celebrate your anniversary, my brother used to…"

- This is also an opportunity to let someone know how important they were to the person who died. You can do this by saying, "I remember how much Mom loved being with you. Can you share some stories with me of the times you spent together?"

Join us in the video library for more on this approach to converting grief to mourning. http://bit.ly/HMHLVideoLibraryLink

26
Keeping a Memory Book

When our loved one dies, we find our hearts and minds fill with stories. These are the stories that make up the life of our loved one. We become the keepers of their story. Stories and images cycle in our minds, stirring up emotions, desperate for an outlet and an opportunity to influence and inspire. Releasing those memories to paper and compiling the stories for future generations is a beautiful way to honour their memory and create a family heirloom.

A memory book provides a repository for our memories, pictures and feelings. The creation of the memory book gives everyone an opportunity to participate and include their stories. In this way, a memory book can provide a healing opportunity for everyone who participates. As we share the stories, so do we convert more of our grief to mourning.

On the one-year anniversary of my mother's passing, I returned to her home for a tree planting ceremony. I brought along a remembrance book and asked anyone who was willing, to record a story about their time with my mother. I learned things about my mother I might not otherwise have known. To this day, when I miss her, I open the book and read. It warms my heart and I don't feel so alone. I also now have a precious gift to share with her grandchildren.

Getting Started

- Find a book that speaks to you. There are a number of them on the market. Some have beautiful sayings and peaceful pictures. I managed to find one in my Mom's favourite colour.

- Invite friends and family to share their stories. There are two ways to include their stories in the book:

  - You can write the story based on what you remember of what they said.

  - You can ask them to write the story. In a time of grief, it is often much easier to ask someone to write the story for you than to do it yourself. When someone asks you what they can do to support you in your grief, it is a wonderful opportunity to say, please write a story of a time you shared with my beloved.

  - When you receive the email or the card with the story in it, it is very easy to print and paste the story into the book.

- The book can be shared with family and friends. It is amazing how stories beget stories. As you share the book, you will likely find that even more stories come forward.

- As you ask for these stories, you provide a pathway for the other person to convert some of their grief to mourning.

Join us in the video library for more on this approach to converting grief to mourning. http://bit.ly/HMHLVideoLibraryLink

27

Soundtrack of Our Life Together

As we work through our grief, we may discover that the pop songs or other musical pieces that once triggered sudden bursts of overwhelming grief now also prompt a smile. The pain has softened and given way to more joyful memories. Now, the tears are as much about gratitude for having the memory, as they are for no longer having the person here to share it with. The music has become a comfort and an important healing tool, forever bringing us back to particular moments and anchoring that time in our memory.

When my Godfather died, I spent time in his apartment gathering and packing things for my Godmother. A Carpenters concert was on the TV the entire time I was in their apartment. It reminded me of the songs that were on the radio when I was a child dancing in the kitchen with him to the sound of the radio. A few months later, as I was driving, a Carpenters song came on the radio. I was immediately transported to that day with all of its sadness and heartache. Even now, years later, when a Carpenters song comes on, I remember that day, but instead of the sadness, a smile comes to my face. I remember my Godfather and all the wonderful times we shared.

With time and conscious work to convert the grief to mourning, the symptoms of grief soften and we can reclaim our wonderful memories and the joy our loved one brought to our life. Music is a terrific way to convert grief to mourning and to gauge our progress in the healing journey.

Getting Started

- ♥ Make a list of songs that remind you of your loved one. These can be songs

    - ♡ They loved.

    - ♡ You associate with them.

    - ♡ Remind you of them.

- ♥ Create a playlist of your favourite songs from the ones listed above.

- ♥ Listen to the playlist when you miss them and want to reconnect. This will help you to access memories, and with the memories, access both the tears and the laughter.

Join us in the video library for more on this approach to converting grief to mourning. http://bit.ly/HMHLVideoLibraryLink

28
Travel to a Sacred Space

Travelling to sacred spaces gives us time and opportunity to be present with our grief journey. It is essential that we have time to be with our thoughts and feelings. Society encourages us to keep busy and not think about our loss. We may even choose to distract ourselves with busyness. When we take time to get away, we have an opportunity to find quiet and stillness. All symptoms of grief ask us to slow down so that we can be present with our grief and convert it to mourning. By taking the time to go to a special place, we honour this deep need. The travel need not be expensive; it need only be intentional and mindful.

When you take this kind of journey, the opportunities for healing show up everywhere. Four months after my mother died, I went on a European trip that was booked before she became ill. One of the hardest things I ever did was get on the plane. I was feeling anxious and weepy; I was exhausted, and it was the last thing I really wanted to do. By the time I got on the plane, I was a wreck. I sat in my seat and began to weep. I chose to ask myself what this was all about. And I heard a whisper from deep inside, "You're untethered. When this plane takes off, there will be nothing connecting you to the planet; your mother is no longer there." I was devastated. I wept. Then I journaled. By the time I got to Frankfurt, something had changed. I walked by the room where Mom and I had met the last time I was in this airport and I smiled at the memory. I still felt the pangs, but it had shifted. As we do the hard work of converting our grief to mourning, so do the symptoms soften over time.

It is easy to use travel as a way to avoid grief; this is not what we are talking about. As you can see from my example, you want to bring yourself to the situations, feelings and thoughts that pop up so that you can hear the wisdom they have to offer.

Getting Started

- There are many wonderful movies of grief journeys that may inspire you:

    - "Murphy's Law," the documentary of a woman who follows in her father's bike tracks as she recreates his tour of Ireland.
    - "The Way," the story of a father who finishes the journey his son began on the Camino de Santiago.

- Choose a place that had meaning for your relationship. It may be someplace local, a day trip or a place that you journeyed to together. Trust your inner wisdom to direct you to the right place.

- A travel journal can help you reflect on and release what is coming up.

Join us in the video library for more on this approach to converting grief to mourning. http://bit.ly/HMHLVideoLibraryLink

29
Living Their Legacy

It is not uncommon to read in an obituary, "In lieu of flowers, please send donations to …" The causes our loved ones held near and dear tell us something about who they were and what they cared most about. We can learn from family, friends and their cheque book what touched their heart. And we can use that information to follow in their footsteps, if we feel so moved.

Completing projects or expanding on work our loved ones were doing at the time of their death can be a wonderful way of converting grief to mourning. As with all things, we need to do this mindfully; otherwise, it becomes a way of avoiding our grief work. We want to make sure that we are not becoming a crusader for a project that keeps us so busy we block out our grief process. It is important to stay present to the emotions that come up as we do the work or write the cheque that will make a difference in someone else's life.

No matter what we choose to do, it must feel true for us to do. We want to maintain balance as we integrate the legacy project or donation. The hope is that in doing these things, we feel connected to what was important to our loved ones and feel peace as we walk for a moment in their shoes.

Early in my hospice career, I had a client who loved watching Downton Abby. As the final season of the show began, she commented that she "would not survive to see the end of it." After she died, I watched the show religiously.

She was in my mind and my heart as I did it. I shed more than a few tears. And I felt that somehow, I was completing something for her as I was doing it.

Getting Started

- ♥ Make a quarterly, bi-annual or yearly practice of writing cheques to organizations that were near and dear to your beloved. While this may not be a practice that continues over time, in the early days of grief, it may be a way to connect with your dearly departed and act on their behalf.

- ♥ Following through on a legacy project may not have anything to do with charity; it may simply be to finish something they had begun – planting a garden, taking a trip, reading a book, finishing a reno project — the possibilities are endless.

- ♥ Bring friends and family together to work for a day on a project or for an organization that was meaningful to your loved one.

  - ♡ Complete a renovation project that they had talked about.
  - ♡ Volunteer on the same day for a charity they cared about.

Join us in the video library for more on this approach to converting grief to mourning. http://bit.ly/HMHLVideoLibraryLink

30
Cooking Their Favourite Foods

Enjoying the life that they enjoyed can help us to feel closer to our loved one. As we invite flavours and aromas of the foods they cooked to be a part of our day, so do we invite the memories. We reclaim these memories as we share stories with our family and friends. Sometimes, we laugh, sometimes, we shed tears, and sometimes, both occur. It's all good healing in the grief journey.

I love cooking the things my mother cooked. After she died, one of the things I brought home were the cookbooks with her writing in them. I found it reassuring to read the words she had written. I found it comforting to smell the aromas created in my kitchen that were reminiscent of the ones from my childhood. My mother was a working mother, and those smells during the weekends and on holidays were precious to me, even then. Now, as I recreate those aromas and flavours, so do I reclaim those memories and remember what it felt like to have her just downstairs. In the privacy of my kitchen, I can feel the pain of the thought that she will never again be one floor away. I can shed the tears or let out the yell of frustration and anger. I hear her voice whisper in her thick Hungarian accent, "remember to close the peppercorn capsule tight or you'll be fishing them out later." There it is, a piece of the new relationship. She will continue to live in my head and my heart. I'm grateful and frustrated at the same time. It's all part of the dance of the grief journey. The good news is that for this moment, I get to console myself with mother's cooking.

Getting Started

- ♥ If your loved one did cook, find their recipe book and start experimenting.

  - ♡ Invite family and friends over for a memorial meal. Ask them to bring their favourite memories.

  - ♡ Hold a pot luck of your loved one's favourite foods and ask everyone to bring something. You may be surprised by what people bring and the stories that come with the dishes.

  - ♡ Invite family and friends to come early and cook with you so that they, too, can learn the recipes and share the stories.

- ♥ If your loved one did not cook, try to recall their favourite meals and the stories they evoke.

  - ♡ Hold a remembrance pot luck of all their favourite foods and ask everyone to come with a story or a memory they connect to that food.

  - ♡ Invite family and friends to eat a favourite meal enjoyed by your loved one at a local restaurant they preferred.

Join us in the video library for more on this approach to converting grief to mourning. http://bit.ly/HMHLVideoLibraryLink

31
Holding Each Other's Tears

Leonardo Da Vinci said, "Tears come from the heart and not from the brain." The pain in our hearts feels like a hole that cannot be filled. We fear that if we begin crying, we will never stop. Worse, our friends and relatives who don't want us to hurt, try to steer us away from our feelings. In truth, tears are the pathway to and through our grief. They are the pathway to our healing. When we are experiencing soul crushing sorrow, it is not our brain that will lead us out of our misery, it is our heart, and the tears that need to be shed.

Several months after my father died, I realized I was not telling people how I was feeling. I was afraid if I was honest, I would tear up and cry, and my crying would never stop. So, on I went, masking my pain and pushing through my day-to-day activities. One weekend, tired from all the to do's I had put off, I broke a glass while loading the dishes. It slipped from my grasp and shattered into countless shards. For a moment I froze. Then I burst into tears. I whispered, "Daddy, help me, please help me." A young girl who was visiting came running. I stepped toward her to keep her away from the glass. She touched me gently and said nothing; she just allowed my tears to fall. She had lost her mother at a very early age and knew the pain I was in. She knew no words would help me here.

As I began to clear away the broken glass, I started having a conversation with my Dad. Somehow, the tears and this young girl's loving understanding had opened up a space. I realized I needed to get comfortable with my tears and I needed to surround myself with others who would also be comfortable with my tears and my sorrow.

Getting Started

♥ Trust yourself with your tears.

When tears come up, allow them to flow. Our bodies naturally know when release is needed. Allowing the tears to flow when they naturally arise creates a rhythm and relationship with our bodies. With time, tears come less frequently and don't last as long.

♥ Find people you can trust with your tears, people who will gently hold you and your tears when you most need to cry.

♡ Someone who will not interfere with your tears.

♡ Someone who is patient and understanding.

♡ Someone who can hold you, if you need to be held, and quietly witness your process.

♡ Someone who can sit quietly with you and recognize the sacredness of your tears.

♡ Someone who creates a safe space in which you can share your tears.

Join us in the video library for more on this approach to converting grief to mourning. http://bit.ly/HMHLVideoLibraryLink

32

Walking a Mile in Their Fun Shoes

Playing our loved one's favourite games, reading the books they loved, going to the places they loved — all of these bring us closer to our loved one because the activities help us understand who they were. As we read a book that our loved one once read and we see their notes in the margin, we begin to understand at a deeper level who they were, and how they thought. In this way, we connect with them on a different level. It is a wonderful way to feel embraced by their energy and discover where our relationship is with them now.

A couple of months after my father died, I couldn't sleep. I was feeling very restless and I remembered a time when I was home from college and couldn't sleep. I was worried and upset, and my father, who discovered I was awake when he went to the bathroom in the middle of the night, grabbed his backgammon set, came over to me and suggested we play. The memory brought both a smile and a tear. I decided to do what he did. I got up and got out my backgammon set. I played for both of us, something he used to do when he was alone. I could hear him kibitzing in my ear. I heard his frustration when I did something he would never do. I heard his pride when I played a move that he taught me. Most of all, I felt him there, with me, late at night. I didn't feel alone anymore. I realized I would always have backgammon thanks to him. And I would always be able to reconnect with him through the game board. What a gift!

Getting Started

- ♥ Ask yourself the following questions:

  - ♡ How did your loved one play and get joy out of life? Come up with three or four things that they used to do that you would either like to do or learn.

  - ♡ What games or sports did your loved one teach you to play and enjoy?

  - ♡ What were their favourite books?

  - ♡ What were their favourite movies?

- ♥ Choose one of the above and allow yourself the time and the space to play the game, read the book or watch the movie.

- ♥ If you do this with a friend, tell them why you want to play this game with them and share your memories with them as you play the game or engage in the sport.

- ♥ If you do this alone, talk aloud with your loved one. Thank them for what you are discovering as you play the game, read the book or watch the movies through their eyes.

Join us in the video library for more on this approach to converting grief to mourning. http://bit.ly/HMHLVideoLibraryLink

33

Words, Glorious Words

Words help us to explore our world and discover our thoughts and feelings when they seem hidden to us. Writing down our thoughts and feelings can help us to put order to the chaos, to understand what is happening inside and explore what is happening on the outside. In releasing our words to the page, so do we convert our grief to mourning.

For those who are not inclined to write, the words of others can help us process our grief. In words that someone else has written we may see snippets of our experience, and it helps us to feel less alone. We connect with them, and we find relief and release for the grief that has been locked inside.

I have journaled since I was a little girl. I remember running up to my room and spending hours writing in my journal. I always seemed to turn to it when I felt lost. And somehow, I found, almost magically, that resolutions would reveal themselves to me when I wrote about my worries and fears. At times, it felt like I was conversing with God. So, every time I suffered a loss — when my grandmother died, when my pet bird died, when I had a broken relationship, when my cat died, when my friend died, when my father died, when I discovered I was a womb twin survivor, and most recently, when my mother died, it seemed only natural to turn to my journal. Sometimes, it was hard to put words to the page. One day, in a journal entry about my mother, I just kept writing, "I miss you so much, I miss you so much, I MISS YOU SO MUCH." Just writing that out helped some of the hurt dissolve.

Getting Started

- ♥ Find a special journal and pen that you designate your grief journal and pen. These are the friends you go to when you need to release and relieve anything that you are holding inside. These pages hold no judgment or consternation, only love.

    - ♡ Don't set down rules about this process. It is important not to pressure yourself with rules about writing every day or for a set amount of time. Write when you feel like it, for as long as you feel like it.

- ♥ Write a poem.

    - ♡ Write about what you are thinking and / or feeling.

    - ♡ Write about what is going on in your body if you are experiencing aches and pains or other symptoms.

    - ♡ Write about what you wish you could have said.

    - ♡ Write about your loved one and what you wish others knew about them.

    - ♡ Write about what you need from your friends and family right now.

- ♥ Google "grief poems" and find a poem that speaks to you. Sit with the words and let them wash over you.

Join us in the video library for more on this approach to converting grief to mourning. http://bit.ly/HMHLVideoLibraryLink

34

Welcoming the Sacred Silence

For many of us, the silence can be a scary place. We do a lot to avoid the silence. We keep radios and TVs on; we call our friends; we stay busy at work and at home — all to avoid the silence. We believe that our memories and emotions live in the silence, and that they will overwhelm us. The good news is, when we allow ourselves to welcome the silence, we discover that the silence is a safe space where we can relax. We learn to trust the silence. We discover that the thoughts, memories and feelings that come to us in this space are sacred. We get to breathe gently and find peace.

In the final weeks of my mother's life, she wanted the TV on all the time. It was hard for me, as I had always appreciated the quiet and the peace of nighttime. However, the closer we came to the end of her life, the more I relied on TV to provide a safe environment where I could rest. As long as the TV was on, I could focus on the familiar voices of the characters; I could stop thinking, let my mind go and fall asleep. This became a habit. It was a year and a half before I realized that what had begun innocently enough had become a coping mechanism that was doing the opposite. It was preventing me from feeling peaceful. It took time and practice to ween myself off this habit. On anxious nights, I still have to remind myself to welcome in the silence. The benefits of choosing silence are undeniable. I always have a deeper and more restful sleep when I go to bed whispering to the silence, "thank you for this opportunity to rest in your sacred arms."

Getting Started

- ♥ Wise words from Albert Einstein: "I think 99 times and find nothing. I stop thinking, swim in silence and the truth comes to me." How can you allow yourself to swim in silence? What does that look like and feel like for you?

- ♥ In the hit Broadway show Hamilton, Alexander Hamilton, after having lost his young son in a duel, laments and sings, "I never liked the silence before." In the song, he talks about habits he has picked up: walking for long periods of time, attending church, sitting on a bench, praying. What do you do to allow the stillness of your being?

- ♥ Create a slow-down ritual that works for you so you can teach your body that when you do this practice, the mind slows down and there is silence in your being. Some things that can work:

  - ♡ Warm beverage (herbal tea, milk, hot cocoa).
  - ♡ Wrapping yourself in a warm blanket and gazing outside.
  - ♡ Soft music.
  - ♡ Warm bath.
  - ♡ Candlelight or a fire (campfire or in the fireplace).

Join us in the video library for more on this approach to converting grief to mourning. http://bit.ly/HMHLVideoLibraryLink

35
Animal Healing

It is miraculous what animals can do to support us in our healing journey. Animals are intuitive, sensitive creatures that know when and how to bring love. Animals help us to reconnect to our hearts because they respond to our hearts. They are present to the moment, sensitive to and aware of the emotions that are in the air. Their desire is to comfort and heal. Accepting the love of an animal can bring us back to our heart and the present moment. Their love can bring us to deeper places of love and healing in ourselves. When grieving, it can be easier to open our hearts to the unconditional love of an animal and receive their warmth, to cherish their desire for kisses and cuddles. If we are animal people, animal comfort may be just what we need most.

My precious cat, Bella, was just a kitten when I left for seven weeks to be with my mother as she was dying. When I returned home, I was tired and depleted physically, mentally, emotionally and spiritually. After a restless night and having had the TV on (noise Bella was not used to), I awoke in the morning from a couple of hours of deep and blissful sleep. I felt Bella at my shoulder, her paw stretching as close to my heart as she could reach. She was purring softly. I could feel her holding my heart and creating an environment of peace. To this day when I am unwell, Bella, now a much bigger girl, comes and leans against my shoulder, reaches over and puts her paw directly on my heart. The soothing, healing energy radiates from her warm paw directly into my heart.

Getting Started

If you have pets at home, watch them and follow their lead.

- ♥ If they want you to sit down with them, do so.

- ♥ If they want to crawl on your lap or bed, let them.

- ♥ If they want to go for a walk, go for a walk with them.

- ♥ If they want to play, play with them — even if you don't feel like it.

 If you don't have a pet or you need more than one animal:

- ♥ Visit a friend with a pet.

- ♥ Go to a park (especially a dog park or a leash-free area).

- ♥ Visit a petting zoo.

- ♥ Spend time in an animal shelter.

- ♥ Visit a ranch and watch which animals come to you. (Horses, in particular, are incredibly intuitive.)

Join us in the video library for more on this approach to converting grief to mourning. http://bit.ly/HMHLVideoLibraryLink

36

Talk with the Ache

Physical aches and pains are par for the course. While on our grief journey we will likely feel aches and pains in many parts of our body. The difference between suffering through this or walking through it with ease and grace is recognizing the truth that symptoms are our body's way of getting our attention. The purpose is to slow us down so that we can hear the message. When we bring our attention to the pain and ask to hear what the source of the pain is, miracles happen, healing begins and suffering is kept to a minimum. It takes a willingness to be present to the ache and the pain underneath.

Six months after my mother's death, I started to develop an ache in my wrists. They were sore. Holding a pen was challenging. They felt locked, like something was blocking them from rotating properly. One night, while I was icing the inflammation, I closed my eyes and asked myself, "Where is the block? Help me to hear." It was quiet in the room. A whisper came back, "What's the point?" I felt a wave of despair wash over me. Tears filled my eyes, and I began to fall into the feeling. As I allowed myself to consciously release the emotional pain, the physical pain began to subside. Both wrists cracked as I rotated them. They were free, and so was I.

Getting Started

- ♥ Recognize the ache is your grief's way of getting your attention.

- Create a time and space where you can have a conversation with the part of your body that is aching.

- Sit quietly and ask earnestly, "Help me to hear and understand what is happening here."

  - Make sure the inquiry is sincere and that you are willing to hear any answer that arises.

  - Talk with the ache, not to it or at it.

    - We tend to do this when we want the physical pain to go away and we begin negotiating with it instead of listening for its wisdom.

    - Gentleness with our words and intentions is important.

- Listen for the whisper, the still quiet voice that knows the truth and is eager to share it with you.

- Allow all emotions that come up to be expressed out of your body in safe and gentle ways.

Please note, if you are experiencing physical pains, visit your doctor. It is always good to make sure that there is no underlying physical cause of your pain.

Join us in the video library for more on this approach to converting grief to mourning. http://bit.ly/HMHLVideoLibraryLink

37
Slow, Deep Breathing

Our grief is constantly asking us to slow down and take a deep breath. In all areas of grief symptoms — physical, mental, emotional, social and spiritual — the function of the symptom is to ask us to slow down. This is difficult in a society that is always pushing us to move faster and process more. The purpose of slowing down is to help us be present to our grief. If we choose not to slow down, we soon discover our grief journey begins to derail. Deep breathing allows us to stay present to the moment and attentive to our grief so that we can convert it to mourning and move through it with ease and grace.

Earlier in this book, I spoke about my first time on a plane after my mother died and how untethered I felt. Sitting in the plane, the only thing I could do at the moment of takeoff was to breathe. I concentrated on my breath, placing my hands on my chest and on my abdomen. Immediately, I felt the pounding in my chest slow down. As I kept concentrating on sending breath to my abdomen, I felt the tension in my body release. Tight shoulders began to relax and lower. My body and mind were slowing down to the pace of my grief, and my grief was being given a space for memories and feelings to co-mingle. This allowed me to begin processing all that was surfacing.

Getting Started

Slow, deep breathing is helpful in all areas of grief response.

- **Physically** – Slow, deep breathing can be directed to any part of the body that is hurting. Put a hand on the area of your body that is tense or hurting and consciously direct breath into your hand.

- **Mentally** – When mind chatter is loud, confusion and/or fogginess takes over. Slow, deep breathing allows the mind to settle and relax. Put one hand on your forehead and your other hand at the back of your head. Close your eyes, breathe into the space between your hands and feel your mind begin to settle.

- **Emotionally** – Regardless of the emotion, you can begin to regulate emotions by breathing into them. Identify the part of your body that is affected by the emotion. Place your hand there and breathe into it. You will feel the emotion soften so that you can begin to process and release it.

- **Socially** – These symptoms of grief are often associated with secondary losses, e.g., friends and/or family who are not able to be supportive and who disappear from our lives. When we feel abandoned, lonely or upset due to these situations, taking time to sit down and do some slow breathing can anchor and ground us.

- **Spiritually** – As the unanswerable questions begin to arise, slow deep breathing allows us to settle into the place of the unknown and find comfort there.

Join us in the video library for more on this approach to converting grief to mourning. http://bit.ly/HMHLVideoLibraryLink

38
Go for a Walk

Walks help. We feel better after a walk because walking clears our head, opens room in our heart, gives us space to breathe and grace to breathe deeply.

The stressors of grief live in our bodies. As toxins gather, muscles begin to stiffen and ache; cortisol and adrenaline levels rise, as does anxiety. Through physical movement those levels drop and balance. As toxins are released, so are anxiety and tension released from the body. In addition to these physical benefits, going outside for a walk connects us to something bigger, something greater than ourselves. As we breathe in the fresh air, we expand our awareness of what is around us and what is supporting us.

Shortly after my father died, I found his walking stick. In my search to find a connection with him, I decided to walk with his stick. I remembered summer holidays when we would spend the first day searching for the perfect size stick for all of us. He would spend that night whittling the handles and the bottoms of the sticks we found. The next day he would invite us to go for walks with him. He was never happier than when walking in the mountains. Walking with his stick soon became a daily habit. I lovingly placed his stick just inside my front door. Every time I left the house, I saw it, and it would call to me. I walked every day. Some days just for 10 minutes; other days for well over an hour. On the odd day when I didn't walk, I found my muscles became sore and stiff. The stick seemed to support me on these walks and throughout my grief journey. There were days when I lovingly caressed the stick and other days when I pounded the stick onto the ground. Whatever emotion I was feeling, the stick could take it from my body and release it into Mother Earth. Mother Earth knew what to do with this energy; I did not.

Getting Started

- ♥ Make a choice to go for a walk. It can be for just 15 or 20 minutes. Let it become a regular practice; the rewards will be great.

- ♥ Find a walking stick that can support you in your journey. It may be a family heirloom, one you borrow from a friend, one you make yourself or one you purchase.

- ♥ Consciously choose your route. Are you going to explore places, streets and pathways that you know well today, or are you going to explore some new place?

- ♥ If you are uncomfortable walking alone, find a walking buddy — someone who will be comfortable with both silence and your stories.

- ♥ Invite others who have similar losses to walk with you. Together, share your experiences and stories. After a 30-45 minute walk, stop for a beverage and continue the conversation.

Join us in the video library for more on this approach to converting grief to mourning. http://bit.ly/HMHLVideoLibraryLink

39
Carving a Story Stick

Many cultural traditions have used a story stick or totem pole to tell the story of a family or an individual. During grief, it is not uncommon to go through a period of review and reflection on our life with our dearly departed. All types of emotions may appear: remorse, guilt, blame, shame, regret, joy, happiness, longing — the possibilities are endless. One way to work through the emotions that come up is to create an object that records and transmutes the energy of the emotions. Carving or decorating a stick is a powerful way to release emotions from our body and transmute them into something beautiful.

As a theatre person, I always knew the power of creativity, storytelling and the talking stick. In the first seven-day retreat I facilitated in 2005, I decided to introduce a daily project. On the first day, I handed out four-foot cedar sticks. Every day, the participants would have designated time to decorate the sticks. They could sand them, carve them, paint them or embellish them. All week, they walked the property with their sticks. For most participants, every free moment became a conversation with their stick. At the end of the week, we introduced our sticks to the group at a special campfire ceremony. We called them the Walk-Your-Talk sticks. They were powerful tools. I was amazed when, the following year, a number of participants returned with their sticks. One of them said she needed to burn her stick to release what was put into it the previous year, and to begin anew with a fresh stick. I have done walk-your-talk sticks at every retreat I have ever facilitated. I have never found a better tool for transferring and transmuting blocked energy.

Getting Started

Create your own walk-your-talk stick.

- ♥ Purchase a four-foot stick of wood from any building supply store. (Cedar has a particularly nice touch and smell.)

- ♥ Use the stick. Walk with it and listen to it as you walk. Feel what it wants you to do. (This builds communication with your stick and with your inner self).

- ♥ Begin to carve a place for your hand. Use files and sandpaper to get it just right (note: this will take a while. Don't be impatient; it is a process.)

- ♥ As you work with the stick, remain mindful of your loved one. Honour the stories, the essence of who they were and who you were together with your stick.

- ♥ Build a walk-your-talk stick supply box. Go browsing in a hobby store and see what catches your eye. You may want to include wood carving tools of different shapes and sizes, different grades of sandpaper, files, paints and brushes, markers, wood glue, glitter glue, feathers, beads, leather strips — anything that speaks to you.

- ♥ When your stick is complete, share the story of the stick with a friend.

Join us in the video library for more on this approach to converting grief to mourning. http://bit.ly/HMHLVideoLibraryLink

40
Make a Sound

If you gave your grief a voice, what would it sound like? In the West, we are taught from an early age to hold it in. It takes a ton of energy to hold that sound in and contain it. Other cultures understand that there is a sound that goes along with the existential fear, the loneliness, the vulnerability and the sorrow that we feel. Being able to tap into the sound and release it offers great relief. In Irish culture, women were brought into a house that was grieving to keen. The keening began with a chant that would bring everyone into a deep heart space. From that heart space, deep, soulful wailing would begin. These guttural sounds would release the angst and pain that the body was carrying.

My first experience of keening occurred one weekend afternoon when I received word that a friend of mine was in a bad motorcycle accident. He had survived; however, he had severe trauma to the head that would result in brain injury if he ever came out of the coma he was in. The phone fell from my hands, I fell to my knees, and the sound that came out of my body felt like it shook the foundation of my house. There was no stopping the sound. It was primal and guttural and just had to be expressed. There were no words attached. I gasped for air and then another belly bomb (that is what it felt like) came through my vocal cords. For a moment, I thought I was going crazy. I just couldn't process the information, and my body was utterly rejecting what it had just heard. After about four minutes of this, I began to recover my breath and to think clearly. Ever since that day, when something happens, I check into my body to see how much I am holding in and whether I need to find a safe way to release it.

Getting Started

There are many ways to release this energy from the body.

- ♥ Go for a walk in the woods and let her rip! It's helpful to have a walking stick with you that you can pound on the ground. Give that energy to Mama Earth; she knows what to do with it!

- ♥ Scream under water. This can be in a hot tub, a swimming pool, a lake or the ocean. The water muffles the sound and you come out feeling like you dropped a tremendous weight from your body. Just remember that sound travels under water, as do vibrational waves. You may not want to do this in a crowded area.

- ♥ Scream into a pillow — the bigger the pillow, the better!

- ♥ The key here is to cut loose and let it go. Remember, whatever we don't allow ourselves to express stays stuck in our body. Over time, this becomes debilitating.

Join us in the video library for more on this approach to converting grief to mourning. http://bit.ly/HMHLVideoLibraryLink

41
In-between Spaces

Sacred spaces are often referred to as thin spaces. These are places where the veil between this life and the life beyond becomes thin. When we are in these spaces, we feel a part of something larger and we are more likely to feel connected with our loved one. For those who have been caretakers of our loved one before they died, we were walking very close to the veil, so we are particularly sensitive to in-between spaces. These places open our hearts and invite us to be present to our thoughts and feelings. Choosing to be in a space that resonates in this way for us can bring comfort. It can also bring up grief that is hiding deep inside. In our everyday world, we don't get the opportunity to be truly present to the depths of our grief. These spaces afford us that opportunity and the grace to move through whatever may arise.

Every time I visit a family grave, I kiss my fingers and place them gently on the gravestone. I close my eyes and imagine my ancestor. I always feel them like a warm embrace. In that embrace, I seem to crumble. Feelings that have been walled up come freely to the surface, and I feel bathed in my own tears, caressed by a gentleness that has wrapped itself around me. I feel connected with my ancestors every day, yet when I am at the cemetery, I feel their presence more closely. These visits are precious to me. They nurture me, sustain me and remind me of the gift of life.

Getting Started

- **Nature** – Whether it is in the mountains, by the ocean, in a forest, in the desert, soaking in hot springs — whatever form of nature speaks to your heart — nature is your truest and deepest connection. Feeling your feet in the water or on the grass connects you to Mother Earth, and through her to something greater.

- **Cemetery or columbarium** – You can feel the sacredness of these spaces when you visit. The veil is very thin here. It is comforting, because you feel closer to your loved one in the final resting place of their physical remains.

- **Sunrise and sunset** – Times of day can also be experienced as in-between spaces. Finding sunrise and/or sunset rituals, such as meditation or yoga practices, can help you feel connected in these sacred times.

- **Build a grief garden** – Create a sacred space of your own where you can be with your thoughts and feelings. A garden is perfect for this, because you can be the architect of the experience that brings you into the in-between space.

  - Smells - plant herbs and flowers that spark memories.

  - Sights – plant colours, textures and add special features.

  - Sounds – add a water feature that trickles, or chimes that come alive with the wind.

Join us in the video library for more on this approach to converting grief to mourning. http://bit.ly/HMHLVideoLibraryLink

42
Meditation

Meditation is an ancient way to calm the nervous system, ease the mind and connect to something greater. During times of grief it can be challenging to achieve these states of peace. While it is true that, during the grief journey, we need to find ways to embrace the discomfort, it is also true that we need to cultivate the tools that remind us how to access peace within ourselves. Finding a meditation practice that works for us becomes an invaluable tool throughout our grief journey.

A year after my mother died, I found a lovely man on Facebook, Lou Martin. Every morning, Sunday to Thursday, Lou would do a Facebook live meditation from Bandon, Ireland. Since he would telecast at 2 a.m. my time, I rarely caught it live. That didn't matter. What mattered was that, whenever I woke up, Lou would be there with his gentle voice. Every morning, I would connect to the half-hour ritual of readings and meditation. Some mornings, I slept through it, and it was always the deepest, most restful sleep. Other mornings, I would hang on his every word. This became a daily ritual for me. It was a way to start the day and know that I was not alone. It was a lifeline. On Fridays and Saturdays, I began developing my own ritual, which continues to this day. I am forever grateful to Lou, whose morning meditations still bring joy and peace to my day.

Getting Started

- ♥ **Guided meditation** – The key to finding a guided meditation that works is to find a voice that you find soothing and a topic that provides what you are looking for. There are guided meditations for better sleep, peace, serenity, forgiveness — the possibilities are endless. Find the topic and voice that work for you. Even if you do not achieve the meditative state, you will still begin to build the pathway to peace of mind and body.

- ♥ **Music meditation** – These meditations have no words, just music and/or nature sounds. Find something soothing. If you can't stop thinking, try a guided meditation first.

- ♥ **Walking meditation** – Going for a walk with the conscious intention to listen to your surroundings and be present is a wonderful way to embrace the moment. This is particularly effective when walking in nature.

- ♥ **Movement meditation** – Select a style of music that suits the movements your body wants to make (at times this can be harsh strong vibrant sounds, at other times soft, gentle, undulating sounds). Put the music on, clear your mind of all thoughts and let your body move through the space, expressing whatever needs to be released. Gabrielle Roth's 5Rhythms is a great way to work with this.

Join us in the video library for more on this approach to converting grief to mourning. http://bit.ly/HMHLVideoLibraryLink

43
Willingness to Be in the Grief Process

Embracing the discomfort of your grief journey is key to healing and moving through it with ease and grace. As a society, we are deeply uncomfortable with sorrow and the expression of sadness. We don't know what to do with it or how to process it so we hide from it, deny it, bury it and carry it, instead of dealing with it. Willingness is everything. The good news is, since every loss and every grief is unique, how we handle it and move through it will be unique, as well. Only our inner selves know the pathway through our grief. What we need to do is become proficient at listening to our inner guidance and be willing to follow where it leads.

Sitting on the sofa one evening, exhausted emotionally and physically, the last thing I wanted to do was more grief processing. "Enough already!" I screamed. "I have nothing left to give." I closed my eyes and heard the following, "What if this tiredness is because you are carrying stuff that is no longer for you to carry? Don't you want to let go of the load?" I did, as long as it could be done in my sleep. "Okay" said my inner voice, "get ready for bed and we'll do the rest." I went straight to bed, which was not my plan. As I climbed the stairs, I felt the heaviness and became present to it. It was in my lower back, my knees and my ankles. Lying down in bed felt good. I put a pillow under my knees to relieve some of the pain. I felt myself sink into the bed. And then I felt something drain from my feet. I fell asleep and awoke two hours later. I was disoriented, because I thought it was the next morning. I jumped out of bed with energy and vigor. It was amazing. Surrendering to the process, whatever that process was, afforded me ease, grace and much needed rest. To this day, when I feel tired, I surrender the fight against it and welcome the process it is connected to.

Getting Started

- ♥ Ask your body what it needs, and follow its directions.

- ♥ Emotions on Your Sleeves – I learned this exercise from Dr. Wolfelt. Both my clients and I have benefitted from doing it. It is a great way to access emotions and work through them.

    - ♡ Get a post-it pad.

    - ♡ Ask yourself what emotions have been part of your grief journey?

    - ♡ Write one emotion on each post-it then place them on your arms.

    - ♡ Pull off a post-it, look at the emotion and think about how it has come up in your grief journey and either talk about it with a friend or journal about it.

Join us in the video library for more on this approach to converting grief to mourning. http://bit.ly/HMHLVideoLibraryLink

44
Borrowed Tears

Borrowed tears are tears that are prompted by an external force. My mother used to say that she needed a "tear jerker," meaning that she needed a movie that was sad and would make her cry. In grief, we carry pent up emotions. We may be aware of them welling up inside, but we do not know how to access them or release them. Movies, books, music and TV shows that allow us to release tears allow us to access those places that seem closed off and hardened. Borrowed tears are needed when we know we need to feel our feelings but can't seem to access them.

As I was headed into the first holiday season without my father, the Christmas commercials began. Usually the hallmark commercials choke me up, but this evening I was taken out by a cell phone commercial. You know, the one where the daughter is leaving on a snowy night and the package her parents gave her begins to ring. It is her father, making sure she is okay. I was a puddle. It felt bad, until it felt good. I started looking for that commercial. A week later, I decided to create a playlist of songs that were special to my father and me so that whenever I needed to release some tears, or just feel close to him, I would have a tool right there. I still cherish that mix and play it whenever I feel called to. "Piece of Sky" from Yentl still elicits tears.

Getting Started

- ♥ Think of movies that you love that have one or more scenes that always make you cry. Movies like Sleepless in Seattle, Steel Magnolias and Terms of Endearment are ideal.

- ♥ Songs are also good for connecting you to your heart centre. You can choose either a song or album that has always had a deep effect on you or songs that hold special meaning and memories for you.

- ♥ TV shows also have the power to engage us with the characters' stories and bring us to tears. Choose one that resonates for you and has brought you to tears in the past.

- ♥ Books tend to be less effective, as you may be having difficulty holding concentration and reading at this time. If it proves frustrating, move on to another example. If you are able to read, you may want to read a story that you have read before.

Note of caution: if you are experiencing a traumatic loss, you do not want to use a story that mirrors your own experience, unless your inner guidance affirms it is okay for you to do so. We do not want to re-traumatize ourselves; what we are looking to do here is release tears that are pent up inside and need a vehicle for expression.

Join us in the video library for more on this approach to converting grief to mourning. http://bit.ly/HMHLVideoLibraryLink

45
Forgiveness

With the death of a loved one comes the regret review. This is when we go through the "coulda, woulda and shouldas." Inevitably, we come up with things that we wish we hadn't done, said, thought or felt. The pain of the blame, shame and/or guilt can compound the feelings of loss and sorrow. Forgiveness becomes our saving grace. While forgiveness can be hard, it is an essential part of the grieving process. Remembering that we are all doing the best we can with the tools and skills we have allows us to forgive ourselves and others. This process can take a long time. It all hinges on our willingness and our compassion.

Ten days after my mother's memorial service, I discovered one of my best friends had died unexpectedly. I was devastated and felt very guilty. I was angry at my friend at the time of her death. Because of the shock of the death, the anger and the guilt got buried. It was a year before the feelings began to resurface. Still not willing to own them, I buried them for another year. On the second anniversary of her passing, I had a back spasm. It was so severe, I lay down on my living room floor. This was something she used to do when she had back spasms. I looked up and saw her picture. In that minute, the feelings of anger, guilt and shame washed over me. As I lay on the floor, I allowed the feelings in, one at a time, and focused on breathing deeply. I said out loud, "I am so sorry. I miss you so." A feeling of forgiveness and peace swept over me. That night, I dreamed of my friend. We were at our favourite coffee shop having a chat like we used to. I told her about the anger and the hurt. She nodded knowingly. I apologized. To my surprise, she also apologized. It was nice to feel her hug again. In the morning, I felt the echo of pain in my back, but the spasms were gone.

Getting Started

- ♥ Ask yourself if you are willing to forgive yourself and/or the other for what occurred?

    - ♡ If yes, look at the suggestions below for pathways to forgiveness.

    - ♡ If no, ask yourself: Are you willing to be willing to forgive?

        - ♥ If the answer is yes, look at the suggestions below.

        - ♥ If the answer is no, ask yourself what it would take for you to be willing to be willing.

- ♥ Ask yourself which of the following pathways to forgiveness is right for you.

    - ♡ Prayer for forgiveness (create your own or seek assistance).

    - ♡ Meditation on forgiveness (guided meditations are great for this).

    - ♡ Writing a forgiveness letter (see Love Letters #46).

    - ♡ Creating your own forgiveness ritual (see The Importance of Ritual #51).

Join us in the video library for more on this approach to converting grief to mourning. http://bit.ly/HMHLVideoLibraryLink

46
Love Letters

My clients often tell me they were advised to write a letter of good-bye, including all the things they never got to say. Clients agonize over this. When I ask them what they want to do, they invariably say, I do want to write a letter, but not to say goodbye. Our insides know saying good-bye is not what we need to do. Most of us long to say the things we never got to say, the expressions of gratitude, forgiveness and love that we want to share. Letters are a pathway to reopen communication with our loved one. Through them, we become able to write the words that weigh on our hearts and release them from our mind and body.

When I was 12, my grandmother, who was also my best friend, was taken to the hospital. She was too sick to talk on the phone. I missed speaking with her every day. I missed her sage advice and her comforting tone. When I didn't know what to do about something, I would write to her about it in my journal. When she died, I was lost. Because I had begun writing to her in my journal, I continued to write to her. My journal became a diary of my letters to my grandmother. The entry always began, "Dear Grandma." Soon, my journal became a place I wanted and needed to go. I would go to it with a heavy heart, and feel better after having written. This was a way for me to begin a conversation with her that continues to this day. When I am feeling lost and not sure what to do, I light a candle, pick up my journal and my pen, and I write. We still have a way to commune.

Getting Started

- ♥ Start with a single letter. Find a special card or stationary.

  - ♡ Create a ritual for the letter writing. Light a candle, brew a cup of tea, light a fire — find what is right for you, so that you feel connected to your loved one as you write.

  - ♡ Write what is in your heart. No one else will see this. This is your opportunity to say what you truly feel. It does not have to be pretty. Sometimes we are angry; sometimes we are hurt or confused. Write it all out.

  - ♡ When you are done, you can choose to keep the letter(s) or you can choose to release them. Many cultures believe that if you burn the letter, the wind will carry your words to your loved one. Again, do what feels right for you.

- ♥ Begin a special journal that is an on-going conversation with your loved one.

  - ♡ As a monologue, you write each entry to your beloved.

  - ♡ As a dialogue you can write questions and responses, allowing your non-dominant had to write the response.

Join us in the video library for more on this approach to converting grief to mourning. http://bit.ly/HMHLVideoLibraryLink

47
Gratitude in Grief

Even in the space of loss there can be a tremendous amount of gratitude in the grief journey. In the expression of that gratitude, so do we experience grace. As we sit with the question "What am I grateful to or for today?" a number of thoughts may come up. What we are doing is beginning to train our brain to look for the things we are grateful for. It is a technique that will support us throughout our grief journey and beyond. We vibrate with what we focus on. When we focus on what we are grateful for, we attract more of the same. One way to lighten the load of grief is to begin to choose our focus and our thoughts.

Half a year after my mother died, having hosted three memorial services, it was now time for me to think about how I was going to pick up and carry on. I had been suffering from all of the normal symptoms of grief. I was still feeling tired, weary, low in energy, easily confused and disoriented. I found relief in meditation when my mind would let me go there. Then, one day, I had an epiphany. I asked myself the question, "What would help me the most right now?" The answer came, "Tell me what you are grateful for." In the following weeks, with the help of the teachings of Dr. Robert Holden (See Journal It – Write It Out #16), I developed the pages of what I would later call my grief gratitude journal. Every day, I answered four basic questions. It became part of my mo(u)rning spiritual practice. It was my lifesaver. To this day, I do this every morning. On the odd day that I forget to do it, or feel I don't have time for it, I feel the difference in my day.

Getting Started

- ♥ What does love want me to know now?

- ♥ What is one way that life is loving me right now?

- ♥ What is one way I could let life love me even more?

- ♥ What are five things I am grateful to or for today? (Sometimes they come right away, and sometimes it takes all day to identify them.)

Join us in the video library for more on this approach to converting grief to mourning. http://bit.ly/HMHLVideoLibraryLink

48
Legacy in Giving

Giving of our time, talents and treasures is a lovely way to keep someone's memory alive. It is said that someone dies three times, first when they stop breathing, second when they are buried and finally when we have forgotten them. This is why finding ways to keep the memory of them alive feels so important. When the one we love left a legacy of giving, following in their footsteps helps us to feel like we are living their legacy. We feel more connected with them and we feel good for our efforts, which also reconnect us with our community.

My mother was always volunteering; her favourite thing to do was to advocate for seniors by serving on the boards of various nursing homes. She also served her community by serving on condo boards. She spent countless hours using her organizational skills to benefit her community. My mother was also very generous, giving annual donations to her favourite charities. When she died, the requests for donation kept coming. I decided to take my time, filter through her favourite charities and find what was true for me. In the first year following her death, I gave to some of her favourite charities in her memory. Since that time, I have decided to spend more time working with the charity I love, Rotary International. My mother's best friend had polio as a child and was in a wheelchair for the rest of her days. With Rotary's commitment to eradicate polio, I felt I was doing what was true for me and carrying my mother's volunteering spirit forward in a way that was meaningful for us both. Giving of my time, talents and treasures is my way of life, because it was her way of life: she taught me well.

Getting Started

- ♥ Obituaries often include lines like "In lieu of flowers, please contribute to…" and you insert some of your beloved's favourite charities. You can extend that thought by initiating annual contributions donated on their birth or death day in their memory.

- ♥ A legacy donation traditionally refers to a donation stipulated in a will to a charitable organization. It is possible to note in your will a gift that is given in memory of and gratitude for your beloved.

- ♥ Identify a talent that your community needs, a talent your loved one noticed in you, and find a way to share that talent to benefit your community.

- ♥ When grieving someone's death, working with young people is a brilliant way to remind yourself of the circle of life.

Join us in the video library for more on this approach to converting grief to mourning. http://bit.ly/HMHLVideoLibraryLink

49
Read a Book

There are countless resources that can support us in our grief journey and beyond. The important thing to remember is that we are the expert on our own grief. Only we know what is right for us. When we find something that feels right, we must pursue it. The early time of grief has a steep learning curve. The person we were when our loved one was alive is no more, and we have yet to discover who we are becoming. We are in a time of exploration, awakening and enlightenment. Books and other resources can help us with this journey. When in doubt, we must trust that we can simply ask for what we need; the universe always responds. Developing a willingness to listen, through our willingness to grieve, helps us to acquire a skillset that makes it easier for us to hear the messages that are being sent to us.

Many books have influenced me over my life. Books are my go-to when I am confused about something or need to learn about something. During my different grief journeys, books have been both a blessing and a curse. In the early stages of grief, it is impossible for me to read. My brain just can't concentrate. I learned this while I was grieving my grandmother and my father. By the time I was grieving my mother, I knew not to even try. I discovered books that I could skim through, or read one page at a time, books like Dr. Wolfelt's *Grief One Day at a Time* were invaluable. I also found great comfort in spiritual texts that I had in the house and had not looked at for years. One day, I felt prompted to stand in front of my bookshelf, a bookshelf I walk by every day and never pay attention to. My eye fell to the book I needed to read. As I pulled it off the shelf, it fell open, and there were the words I most needed to hear. I was reminded anew: when we ask, the answers are given to us.

Getting Started

- ♥ Take a deep breath, close your eyes and ask yourself, what book or resource has the words I most need to hear right now? Listen for the answer. Then connect with the resource. You will be glad you did.

- ♥ Make a list of books that you

  - ♡ find comforting.

  - ♡ enjoy.

  - ♡ have heard about that you would like to read.

  - ♡ find inspiring.

  When you feel in need of support, encouragement, entertainment or inspiration, look at the list you made. Let your eyes drop to the book that would support you the most in this moment.

- ♥ When in doubt, stand in front of your bookshelf and see what title jumps out at you.

Join us in the video library for more on this approach to converting grief to mourning. http://bit.ly/HMHLVideoLibraryLink

50
Honouring the Special Days

Anniversary / Birthday

Special days, be they birthdays, anniversaries, holidays or the anniversary date of the death of our loved one are times when we feel the physical loss more keenly. We imagine what this day might be like if they were still with us. We remember times gone by. On these days, it doesn't matter how many years it has been, it feels like just yesterday when they were here, and we miss them all the more. These days give us an opportunity to be with our grief in a deeper way. They offer us the conscious awareness of the places in our hearts and minds where the memory still carries pain. As we choose to stay present to the pain and shed the tears that spill forth, so do we reclaim another part of the love and the memories that come flooding back as the tears subside. We can giggle at memories of family celebrations, surprises that took our breath away and plans that went awry. These are the moments of our lives. As we reclaim them, one-by-one, they come out of the shadow and instead of causing us pain, we now remember these moments with love.

On what would have been my mother's 82nd birthday (more than two years after her death), I went to her grave and pressed my fingers over her birthdate, which was carved in the stone. I began a conversation with her. "Mom, I miss you. I wish I could celebrate this day with you." And I heard a whisper back, "You are celebrating with me." I laughed out loud. I couldn't help myself. It was true. Of all of the places I could have chosen to be this day, I chose to be here with her and with my memories. In the quiet of the cemetery, and after much conscious work, I was able to smile and give gratitude for this beautiful lady and the many years I was blessed to share with her.

Getting Started

Ways to celebrate special days to bring meaning and consciousness to the day:

- ♥ Plan to spend some time in a sacred place that brings you close to your loved one and the memories you have of them.

- ♥ Choose traditions that have meaning for you and decide how you will incorporate them into your day.

- ♥ Plan a special meal and invite people who have memories to share with you.

- ♥ Imagine that you are having a very special family dinner. You get to invite anyone, living or dead. What would you say to them? Write each attendee a letter. Pour what is in your heart onto the page. This is a wonderful way to release what you have been carrying. You need not send the letters to those who are living. You get to decide what you want to do with each letter.

Join us in the video library for more on this approach to converting grief to mourning. http://bit.ly/HMHLVideoLibraryLink

51
The Importance of Ritual

Dr. Wolfelt reminds us that "Ritual is what we do when we have no words." There are times throughout our grief journey when words fail us. That is the time for ritual. Ritual transmutes the unbearable. It provides space and grace to digest the indigestible and offers new perspective as we surrender to the transmutation that occurs. A ritual can be created for any situation or circumstance. The important part of ritual is that it has meaning for the person or people participating in it. We get to create what has meaning for us. As we take the time to consider what would be meaningful, reflect on what is important to us and concretize the action steps, so do we take the healing steps necessary. Ritual allows us to be with and move through our sorrow and longing.

I created three rituals for my mother after she died. The first was a celebration of her life in Seattle, on what would have been her 80th birthday. It was an opportunity to go through pictures and tell her story to friends who had known her for 15 years, but did not know her life's story. The second, in Windermere, was the burial of her ashes and my parent's wedding rings on their wedding anniversary. The final, in New York, on the five-month anniversary of her death was for family and friends. The rituals helped the people she loved connect with one another. We all needed this time together. Together, in three communities that she loved dearly, we mourned her passing and took another step in our grief journey.

Getting Started

♥ Grief is not a one and done. Rituals will be required throughout your grief journey. They allow your grief to ebb and flow, so that you can smile and laugh when it feels true to do so, and when it is time to cry and release, you are available to that, as well. When you have no words, creating a ritual will bring you present to the moment and allow the grief journey to continue.

♥ There is no such thing as too many rituals, we do as many as we need.

♥ It is never too late to create a ritual, we do what we can, when we can. All in right and perfect timing.

♥ Throughout this book I have given you ideas of ways to ritualize your grief experience so that you can find where the relationship lives now and transmute your pain to the experience of love. It is my hope that you will mix and match what you have found here to suit your individual needs and the needs of the situation(s) as they arise.

♥ Set a clear intention to create something that has deep meaning for you and listen to your inner guidance. All answers live inside you.

Join us in the video library for more on this approach to converting grief to mourning. http://bit.ly/HMHLVideoLibraryLink

52
Venturing Out of Our Comfort Zone

Grief can become its own comfort zone. We are in a protected cocoon of our own making. Eventually, however, we need to begin bursting out of our cocoon. Butterflies know that they need to push themselves out of their protective shell. No one can do it for them. Their wings are made strong from the struggle to get out. If they are cut out of their cocoon prematurely, they will never fly. So it is with us. The time comes for us to venture out of our comfort zone. Like the butterfly, we will know when the time is right. We can trust our instinct with this. Trouble occurs if we feel called from the inside to step out and we allow our fears to hold us back. After a death, we feel fragile and vulnerable. The death has opened us to our inner depths. We have discovered our soft places and we have uncovered strengths we never knew we had. The death has shed a light on our life. If we walked the grief journey well, we have discovered a new norm. Things that used to be true are no longer true. Habits that no longer serve us feel awkward and fall away, and a new way of being with new possibilities and opportunities begins to emerge. Our grief symptoms have softened over time and though we still feel the loss, we feel more confident about how to handle those moments of pain. We welcome the grief burst, because we recognize it is a part of the grief and a testament to our love. We have learned to trust our inner guidance and we have begun to get curious about where it will lead next.

Prior to my mother's passing, I had just completed outlines for two books. They would be my first books published. My wise mentor told me the books would need to be put on hold now. It would not be right to use those books as a way to avoid my grief. He was so right. A year and a half after her death, I contacted him to let him know I was returning to writing, except that there was a book I needed to write before I could return to the other outlines. This is that book. He encouraged me, and here we are. The other two books will be better for the journey I have been on with this one. And so, my wings were forged through the experiences and the writing. What is calling you forward? What will strengthen your wings for flight?

A Meditation

- Think back to your early days of grief. Watch yourself from the outside. Remember the moments that prompted you to build the cocoon.

- Breathe deeply.

- Remember being in the cocoon. Remember the thoughts and the feelings. They may feel like a distant memory, or they may seem like just yesterday. What helped to soothe those moments? What helped to release the pain and reclaim the love?

- Breathe deeply.

- Begin to feel grateful for how far you have come since those early days. Feel grateful to and for your wellness team. Let the gratitude wash over you.

- Breathe deeply.

- Ask yourself what your next steps might be. Allow the question to linger in your mind.

- Feel the awakening from the inside.

Join us in the video library for more on this approach to converting grief to mourning. http://bit.ly/HMHLVideoLibraryLink

Final Thoughts

The grief journey is a sacred one. It is the journey that allows you to reclaim your memories, the joy you felt when you were with your loved one and the love that will be with you always. We honour our loved ones by rediscovering our joy in life and living every day to the fullest. It is my hope that this book has helped you and will continue to remind you how to convert your grief to mourning when the grief bursts come. There will come a time when the grief burst will be a joyful experience, a moment of reconnection and remembering. Your life is a testament to the love in your heart and is part of your beloved's legacy. Live it well. Namaste.

Conversion Technique Comparison Chart

			Symptoms of Grief					Stages of Grief		
Chap	Page	Title	Physical	Mental	Emotional	Social	Spiritual	Early	Middle	Late
1	1	Symbol of Strength	●	●	●	●	●	●	●	●
2	3	Colour My World		●	●		●	●	●	●
3	5	Picture This		●	●	●		●	●	●
4	7	Sleepless and Restless	●	●	●		●	●	●	●
5	9	Linking Objects		●	●	●	●	●	●	●
6	11	Hounour and Altar		●	●		●	●	●	
7	13	Burning Candles		●	●		●	●	●	●
8	15	Creating Your Wellness Team	●	●	●	●	●	●	●	●
9	17	Phone A Friend	●	●	●	●	●	●	●	●
10	19	Importance of Nap Time	●	●	●		●	●	●	
11	21	Permission to Dose	●	●	●		●	●	●	
12	23	Connect with What Connects Us			●		●	●	●	●
13	25	Our Story In Song		●	●	●	●	●	●	●

Conversion Technique Comparison Chart

			Symptoms of Grief					Stages of Grief		
Chap	Page	Title	Physical	Mental	Emotional	Social	Spiritual	Early	Middle	Late
14	27	Going through the Stuff - A Treasure Hunt	●	●	●			●	●	
15	29	Words To Live By		●	●	●		●	●	
16	31	Journal It - Write It Out	●	●	●	●	●	●	●	●
17	33	Message in a Bottle			●		●	●	●	
18	35	Messages and Meaning			●		●	●	●	●
19	37	Drumming the Heartbeat	●	●	●	●	●	●	●	●
20	39	Take Your Loved One to Tea or Coffee			●				●	●
21	41	The Healing Nature of Water	●	●	●			●	●	●
22	43	The Challenge of Holidays			●	●		●	●	●
23	45	Permission to Create a New Holiday Tradition		●	●	●	●	●	●	●
24	47	A Dinner To Remember			●	●		●	●	●
25	49	Connecting with Family and Friends			●	●		●	●	●
26	51	Keeping a Memory Book			●	●		●	●	●

Conversion Technique Comparison Chart

Chap	Page	Title	Physical	Mental	Emotional	Social	Spiritual	Early	Middle	Late
				Symptoms of Grief					Stages of Grief	
27	53	Soundtrack of Your Life Together			●			●	●	●
28	55	Travel to a Sacred Space			●	●	●		●	●
29	57	Living Their Legacy		●	●	●		●	●	●
30	59	Cooking Their Favourite Foods			●	●			●	●
31	61	Holding Each Other's Tears			●	●	●	●	●	●
32	63	Walking A Mile In Their Fun Shoes			●	●	●		●	●
33	65	Words, Glorious Words	●	●	●	●	●	●	●	●
34	67	Welcoming Sacred Silence	●	●	●		●	●	●	●
35	69	Animal Healing	●	●	●	●	●	●	●	●
36	71	Talk With The Ache	●		●			●	●	●
37	73	Slow, Deep Breathing	●	●	●	●	●	●	●	●
38	75	Go For A Walk	●	●	●	●	●	●	●	●
39	77	Carving A Story Stick		●	●	●	●	●	●	●

Conversion Technique Comparison Chart

Chap	Page	Title	Symptoms of Grief					Stages of Grief		
			Physical	Mental	Emotional	Social	Spiritual	Early	Middle	Late
40	79	Make A Sound	●		●			●	●	●
41	81	In-Between Spaces			●		●	●	●	●
42	83	Meditation	●	●	●		●	●	●	●
43	85	Willingness To Be In The Grief Process	●	●	●	●	●	●	●	●
44	87	Borrowed Tears			●			●	●	●
45	89	Forgiveness	●	●	●	●	●	●	●	●
46	91	Love Letters			●		●	●	●	●
47	93	Gratitude In Grief			●		●	●	●	●
48	95	Legacy In Giving			●	●			●	●
49	97	Read A Book			●		●		●	●
50	99	Honouring the Special Days			●	●	●	●	●	●
51	101	The Importance of Ritual			●	●	●	●	●	●
52	103	Venturing Out of Our Comfort Zone								●